POGBA
MBAPPÉ
GRIEZMANN

POGBA MBAPPÉ GRIEZMANN

LUCA CAIOLI
&
CYRIL COLLOT

ICON

First published in the UK in 2019
by Icon Books Ltd, Omnibus Business Centre,
39–41 North Road, London N7 9DP
email: info@iconbooks.com
www.iconbooks.com

Sold in the UK, Europe and Asia
by Faber & Faber Ltd, Bloomsbury House,
74–77 Great Russell Street, London WC1B 3DA
or their agents

Distributed in the UK, Europe and Asia
by Grantham Book Services,
Trent Road, Grantham NG31 7XQ

Distributed in Australia and New Zealand
by Allen & Unwin Pty Ltd, PO Box 8500,
83 Alexander Street, Crows Nest, NSW 2065

Distributed in South Africa
by Jonathan Ball, Office B4, The District,
41 Sir Lowry Road, Woodstock 7925

Distributed in India by Penguin Books India,
7th Floor, Infinity Tower – C, DLF Cyber City,
Gurgaon 122002, Haryana

Distributed in Canada by Publishers Group Canada,
76 Stafford Street, Unit 300
Toronto, Ontario M6J 2S1

Distributed in the USA
by Publishers Group West,
1700 Fourth Street, Berkeley, CA 94710

ISBN: 978-178578-518-4

Typeset in New Baskerville by Marie Doherty

Printed and bound in Great Britain
by Clays Ltd, Elcograf S.p.A.

About the authors

Luca Caioli is the bestselling author of *Messi*, *Pogba*, *Griezmann* and *Mbappé*. A renowned Italian sports journalist, he lives in Spain.

Cyril Collot is a French sports journalist. He is the author of several books and documentaries about French football, and the bestselling biographies *Griezmann*, *Pogba* and *Mbappé*.

Contents

Introduction

The party belongs to those who write history. On the pitch of the Luzhniki Stadium in Moscow, Antoine Griezmann, drenched by the Russian downpour, shows the star off, smiling, pointing at his brand new jacket, fresh out of the packet. Next to him is Kylian Mbappé, the revelation, pointing at what he too had always dreamed of. There was no demonstration of excessive joy but a broad smile and an initial reaction on French television that speaks volumes about him as a person: 'The road was long, but it's been worth it. We're world champions and we're very proud. We wanted to make people happy and that's why we've done all this.'

Paul Pogba's mother, Yeo Moriba, is one of the first to hug her son. His brothers Florentin and Mathias join the party and the four have a family photo taken in La Pioche's favourite pose.

In the dressing room, Benjamin Mendy – with his shirt off – and an overexcited Paul Pogba teach President of France Emmanuel Macron – drenched and missing his tie – to 'Dab'. The scene would be immortalised on social media by Paul's Instagram account. Other moments of glory punctuated the evening, such as

Pogba wearing a Mexican sombrero, speaking perfect Spanish and even performing a tongue-in-cheek version of England's 'Football's Coming Home' anthem.

On 16 July, he strode across the tarmac at Roissy-Charles de Gaulle airport holding the World Cup. The new champions travelled by double-decker bus to the Élysée Palace, where Macron was waiting for them. After the President's speech, it was time for the Pogba show to begin. Relieved of his tie, with the top button of his shirt undone and round sunglasses on his nose, Paul took the microphone and unleashed the master of ceremonies within him. He got the 3,000 people gathered at 55, Rue du Faubourg Saint-Honoré jumping, singing and dancing by chanting: 'We beat them all!', kidding around with Benjamin Mendy, leading a chorus of N'Golo Kanté's name and asking the audience to do Grizou's 'Take the L' dance. Paul Pogba in his purest state.

Pogba, Mbappé, Griezmann.

In other words: Paul, Kylian, Antoine.

Three musketeers for the second star. But how have they come so far?

Chapter 1

Mâcon, Roissy-en-Brie, Bondy

A small provincial town with just over 35,000 inhabitants, about 60 kilometres from Lyon, Mâcon is somewhere not necessarily used to attention. From a sporting perspective, there have not been many champions to speak of, or at least no one like Antoine Griezmann, who was born there in 21 March 1991.

Alain Griezmann, his father, had been a municipal employee for a number of years, so the family – Alain, Antoine, his mother Isabelle, his sister Maud and his younger brother Theo – lived in a small detached home next to the Les Gautriats community centre. It was a working-class neighbourhood, bordered by large pine trees and wide-open green spaces.

Georges Brassens Primary School, an imposing building surrounded by a huge tarmac playground with faint markings for a football pitch, is located in the middle of the neighbourhood, on Rue de Normandie. At school, as he himself admits, Antoine was always at the back of the class, usually chatting: 'I was the kind of kid who would cut bits off my rubber to throw at my friends, and whenever my mother asked if I had any homework, funnily enough I never did!'

'He was a simple, likeable kid who never caused any trouble,' remembers his former headmaster, Marc Cornaton. 'He was one of a group of boys and girls who played football at every break time. After school, it was football again.' As he himself admits, Antoine had his routine at Les Gautriats, kicking the ball alone against the blue doors of the family garage, as well as playing in the basketball court below the house: 'Even when we went to visit my parents' friends I had to take my ball with me. Above all, football was fun, a real passion. When you're ten years old, being a professional is just a dream, nothing more.'

'God had not blessed my brother Fassou with children. He was living in France and was 50, so he returned home to sacrifice a ram in the hope of finding fertility.' This is what Kébé, one of Fassou Antoine Pogba's sisters, told journalist Alban Traquet in March 2017. 'He then left again for Conakry in search of a romantic relationship.'

This trip marked the starting point for the meeting between the Christian, Fassou Antoine and the future mother of Paul Pogba, a Muslim woman in her twenties named Yeo Moriba. Like her future husband, she was from Forested Guinea. Despite the age difference, the ram sacrifice was not in vain. Yeo Moriba gave birth to two beautiful boys, Florentin and Mathias, on 19 August

1990. The small family would spend two years in the port city of Conakry before leaving the Guinean capital to settle permanently in France.

The couple and their two children took possession of an apartment in the Le Bois-Briard development in a peaceful area to the north-east of Roissy-en-Brie, about 30 kilometres to the south-east of Paris. Just one year later, on 15 March 1993, Paul Labile Pogba came into the world at the maternity unit in Lagny-sur-Marne hospital.

When he was only two years old, Paul's parents decided to separate and Yeo Moriba moved a little further away to live in a modest uncluttered apartment in the neighbourhood known as La Renardière, where she brought up her three sons and two nieces on her own. 'I made a lot of sacrifices. I worked morning and night to support them, so they wouldn't be picked on by their schoolmates, would be happy and could go on holiday,' she tells the journalists who come to interview her in her new well-to-do apartment in Bussy-Saint-Georges (about 30 kilometres from Roissy-en-Brie).

The boys were inseparable, and Paul was a real showman. He liked to dance, sing and play the clown. He soon christened himself 'La Pioche' (The Pickaxe). 'There was an Ivorian actor in a TV series, Gohou Michel, who always said "*La Pioche, il va piocher le village*" [The Pickaxe, he's going to use his pickaxe in the village], "*Pogby La Pioche*". I liked it so even my mother started calling me "La Pioche",' Paul said in 2016. Next came the turn of his two brothers: Florentin, the craziest, would be 'Le Zer'. Mathias, who 'had a back like a gorilla', would be simply 'Le Dos' (The Back). Le Zer, Le Dos and La Pioche soon carved out a reputation for themselves in the neighbourhood.

'School?' Paul's mother is uncompromising for the TV cameras: 'He was a total nightmare at school. He would tease his friends and the girls in his class because he was so high-spirited.' Despite being a little embarrassed, Paul can only confirm: 'It's true, I was a real chatterbox. I couldn't keep still. I had ants in my pants.'

Intelligent; lively; mischievous; a dreamer; nice; hyperactive; unruly; and difficult to manage: this is how some of his teachers describe Kylian Mbappé. He was a boy who couldn't sit still at his desk to listen to his teacher's explanations. 'School was not his priority. Kylian had one idea in his head and that was becoming a professional footballer,' says Jean-François 'Fanfan' Suner, AS Bondy technical director and one of Kylian's first coaches.

Born on 20 December 1998 and christened with the name Kylian Sanmi (short for Adesanmi, 'the crown fits me' in Yoruba), he was the first child of Fayza Lottin and Wilfrid Mbappé, who lived on the second floor of a white building at number 4, Allée des Lilas, a five-storey 1950s council building in the centre of Bondy. Fayza – 24 years old at the time and originally from Algeria – grew up in Bondy Nord, in the Terre Saint Blaise neighbourhood. She played handball on the right wing for AS Bondy in Division 1 in the late 1990s and used to work as an instructor in the Maurice Petitjean and Blanqui neighbourhoods. Wilfrid, also an instructor, was 30 when he met Fayza; he was born in Douala in Cameroon and had come to France in search of a better life. First Bobigny, then Bondy, a suburb to the north-east of Paris, nine kilometres from the city's Porte de Pantin, where he worked and played football for years.

'He was a good player, a number 10 who was fond of keeping the ball,' according to Fanfan. 'When he stopped playing, he came back to us and we offered him a coaching position.' One player in particular attracted his attention: he was eleven years old and had arrived from Kinshasa. The boy was called Jirès Kembo-Ekoko; he was the son of Jean Kembo, a midfielder for the Zaire team that become the first team from sub-Saharan Africa to qualify for the World Cup in 1974. Wilfrid was Jirès first coach in 1999 and soon also became his legal guardian; the Lamari-Mbappé Lottin family did not adopt him but Jirès went to live with them and soon became Kylian's big brother, role model, idol and first footballing hero.

Chapter 2

Kicking a ball for the first time

'As soon as he started walking he had a ball at his feet. He spent his free time doing keepie uppies,' remembers Christophe Grosjean, a friend of the Griezmann family and one of his first coaches. For Antoine it was all about playing. 'He was only interested in waiting for break time so he could go outside and play football,' remembers his childhood friend, Jean-Baptiste Michaud.

His pitches were all over the town, at the foot of the tower blocks at La Chanaye, near his grandmother's house: 'People in this part of town remember Antoine as a little blond kid who wore French national team shorts,' recalls André de Sousa, another childhood mate. 'When we were three or four, his parents would take him to visit his grandmother, who lived on the floor below us, and we would take the opportunity to have a kick about. Well, I say "take the opportunity"; he would force me to play with him!'

For the start of the 1997–98 season, Antoine officially received his first French Football Federation licence at the Entente Charnay-Mâcon 71, later Union du Football Mâconnais (UFM). 'We started him at five and a half', confirms his first coach Bruno Chetoux. His father trained a team at the club and Antoine was always hanging around the pitches. To start with, we would only let him train because he was still too young to take part in Saturday matches. But eventually we had him play a few matches before he turned six.' Unsurprisingly, Antoine took to it like a duck to water and attended every session without fail.

'We could see straight away that he was a good player,' explains Chetoux. 'But the most surprising thing was that at that age gifted children tend to be more selfish with their play. Not him, he liked to score goals, but he was also happy to help others score.'

Antoine soon joined the group born a year earlier, in 1990, quickly found his feet and showed himself to have the mindset of a true champion: 'We didn't lose many matches, hardly ever. When it did happen, it was a big deal. I remember an indoor tournament that we lost on penalties. Antoine missed his last attempt. He left in tears, without even waiting for the prize-giving. That showed me his temperament.'

It was always the same. Yeo Moriba had to raise her voice: 'Hey, boys! It's time to come in! Hurry up,' she shouted from her window on the twelfth floor of the tall white tower, using her deep, strident voice to make herself heard. Florentin, Mathias and Paul eventually finished their match, picked up their ball and ran up alleyway no. 13 at the Résidence La Renardière.

Paul was seven years old; Mathias and Florentin were ten. The City Stade had just been built at the end of the playground, along the railway track. It quickly became a rallying point for all the local kids. No prisoners were taken in this rough street football; the boys played right up against the walls and would even hit each other during one-on-ones. Paul was often knocked to the ground. Whenever a tear began to appear in the corner of his eye, he was immediately called to order: 'Stop crying and play!' his brothers commanded. As the matches went on, he became stronger and made progress.

The kid had character alright, as well as a marked taste for competition, something it was said he got from Fassou Antoine. The boys' father took the activity very seriously and whenever the children came to visit, he would give them special sessions on a small dirt pitch near his apartment in Le Bois-Briard.

Paul joined US Roissy in September 1999, following in the footsteps of his two brothers. Sambou Tati, his first coach, remembers: 'I was 30 when I coached Paul's generation for the first time … He was a kid like any other, except you could already see how gifted he was. When he played on the neighbourhood pitches, he scored goal after goal.'

How did his first training session go? 'He was impressive,' comments Sambou Tati. 'Paul likes to say that he scored two or three goals that day. To be frank, I don't remember, and it's difficult to say because at that age the goals are made from cones without a crossbar … One thing for sure is that he had no fear. He wanted to dribble all the time, keep the ball and shoot from anywhere on the pitch. He was a bit selfish, but he was only six years old.'

'He was here every day, always with his father, who was the technical director for the categories from U11 to U17. Kylian must have been three or four years old,' remembers Athmane Airouche, the president of AS Bondy since June 2017. 'He was the club's little mascot. You would see him come into the dressing room holding a ball and sit in the corner, in silence, to hear what the manager had to say before the game. And because Kylian has always been a sponge … from an early age he assimilated football concepts that others only heard and understood years later.'

At aged six, Kylian would finally be allowed to enrol at AS Bondy. His first coach was his dad, a man Airouche would describe as: 'Generous, a hard-worker and fair. Like Fayza, his wife. I can only think of them together because they're like two halves of a whole.' Antonio Riccardi, who has been at AS Bondy for twelve years, first as a player, now as head of the U15s, adds: 'I remember Kylian at four years old, singing the 'Marseillaise' with his hand on his heart or when, at six or seven, he would tell you not to worry and that someday he would be playing for the national team in the World Cup. All you could do was smile, when he was seriously planning out his future: Clairefontaine, the France team, Madrid. We just thought he was a dreamer,' claims Riccardi.

'His idol was Cristiano Ronaldo. He wallpapered his room with posters of the Portuguese player. He liked his dribbling and would watch him on television and try to repeat it on the pitch.' But the five-time Ballon d'Or winner was not the only star Kylian admired. There was also Ronaldinho and Zidane. His childhood friends still make fun of him for the time he showed up at the hairdressers and asked, in all seriousness, for the same style as Zizou. Years later, Kylian would try to justify it: 'When you like a player, you want to do everything just like them. Back then, I didn't know it was baldness!'

Chapter 3

Child's play

Antoine was quickly moved up a category and joined the U13 group trained by Christophe Grosjean for the 2000–01 season. 'That first year, he didn't really manage to hold his own because physique counts for a lot, and at that age he wasn't ready in that respect. But by the second year, he had begun to get bigger physically and better technically. We were still playing in teams of nine and I liked to put him on one side in the centre left position.'

At that time, Antoine spent almost every waking moment with his two best friends, Stéphane Rivera and Jean-Baptiste Michaud. They had no trouble rounding up local kids to make up teams for breakneck matches: 'We imagined we were playing in the World Cup or the Champions League … When we scored, we would try to celebrate our goals in the most original way possible. It was 2002, so Antoine was fond of sliding like Thierry Henry or Fernando Torres,' recalls Jean-Baptiste Michaud.

Despite being vertically challenged, Antoine was one of the most promising players in the Saône-et-Loire *département* in his age category. Paul Guérin, who has been the FFF's Regional Technical Adviser for Burgundy since 2000, had been following the boy from Mâcon closely for several years. 'He was an engaging kid and everyone liked him. He was also incredibly passionate.'

'At twelve and thirteen he distinguished himself every year in the Foot Challenge,' continues Guérin. This competition involved a series of keepie uppies and technical challenges. Antoine was a finalist in 2003, his first year, and won it the following year. In 25 years, only two other players from Burgundy had equalled this and both attended the prestigious Olympique Lyonnais training academy. But Antoine would never have the opportunity to wear the shirt of his favourite club.

From the U10s onwards, Paul was clearly a cut above his teammates. 'We had a fantastic generation,' remembers Papis Magassa, one of his coaches. 'Paul was the individual player who often tipped the match in our direction.' The problem was that his attitude at school was not to Fassou Antoine's liking. 'Sometimes, he didn't turn up at training so we would call his mum to make sure he was okay. In the end it would turn out that his father had punished him. He was tough but fair with him. Paul could cry for hours, but he would never go back on his decision.'

The 2005–06 season, his seventh at the club, was looming. In the U13 category, Paul was reunited with his first coach, Sambou Tati: 'I put him in as playmaker.

I spent my time telling him to play more simply and to stop showboating, but he didn't listen to me. So once I gave him an ear bashing at half-time: "Paul, you're not Ronaldinho, you're crap, you're not the star in this team, you're bringing nothing." He started crying, but as soon as the second half kicked off, he massacred everyone.'

US Roissy finished third in its league and Paul even made several appearances for the U15s. Scouts from professional clubs began hanging around the pitches but Fassou Antoine was not ready to hear talk of leaving Roissy just yet. 'After such a good season, he couldn't stay with us, so I advised him to join US Torcy,' says Tati. Stéphane Albe, the coach at Torcy, a neighbouring town of just over 20,000 inhabitants, was not surprised by the call. 'Our clubs had always had a good relationship and we knew about Paul's potential.'

For his first year in eleven-a-side football, Paul went straight into the midfield. Usually as a defensive midfielder, but also as a box-to-box midfielder or a number 10: 'It's true that he liked to go a long way out of his position,' confirms Stéphane Albe. 'He already had his own way of coming forward, of breaking through. He was capable of taking out several players with a sidestep and of making an impressive difference ... How many goals did he score like that with us? By picking up the ball before speeding up, getting support from another player and then scoring? It must have been at least a dozen.'

US Torcy gave a good account of themselves in the U14 league. The yellow and reds strung together some good performances and finished 'second or third in the table', according to Albe. 'Paul brought a lot to the team, through his play, of course, but also through his charisma and mindset … He was really popular with his teammates and was a delight to coach.'

What about Kylian Mbappé? 'He was a child like all the others who dreamt of becoming footballers, only he had qualities the others didn't,' says Athmane Airouche. Fanfan goes on to explain: 'I had him for a year when he was playing above his age category in the U10s. At training, you could see right away that he had a technical ease. We knew he would go right to the top if there weren't any physical glitches.'

'He made the difference,' adds Antonio Riccardi. 'Quickly, very quickly, like he was a senior playing at a high level, he understood how to shake off his marker, how to get free for his teammates. What was his best quality? His pace with the ball at his feet.'

'He was capable of scoring 50 goals a season in the U13s', remembers Théo Suner, who played with Kylian in almost every category at AS Bondy. 'We didn't even count the goals. He could score three in one game and provide two assists. Kylian was a good friend, he was fun and always smiling.' And Fanfan adds another memory, perhaps one of the best about the lively little kid in a green and white shirt with the number 10 on his back.

'We were playing an important game against Bobigny. It was 0–0 at half-time and we were all over the place. I spoke to the players and told them: "Listen, we're not going to get worked up today. It's simple, in the second half, we're just going to give the ball to Kylian. That's it." We won 4–0 and he was the one who scored the goals.'

Chapter 4

Spotted

'When he was thirteen, he was a little scrap of a thing compared to the others, but he got away with it because of his technical touch. That's what makes the difference now, but back then you couldn't see that yet. He went for plenty of trials at training academies but got knocked back every time because he was too small.' In April 2014, in a TV interview for Basque television, Alain Griezmann remembered the difficult path his son had faced. The 2004–05 season had left its mark; during that year, Alain Griezmann drove him to his various commitments across France but they faced rejection after rejection.

'I went to see him several times,' recalls Alain Duthéron, Olympique Lyonnais' scout in Burgundy. 'He had extraordinary qualities and skill. He wasn't like a centre forward but was a very technical and talented player.' In no particular order he reported: above average technical skill, a very impressive left foot, team spirit and a fantastic insight into the game. In the negative column, he noted: a right foot that was still somewhat lacking and that he was a late developer from a physical perspective, plus his parents were both barely over 5 feet 6 inches.

Competition was already fierce in Lyon. As for players born in 1991, OL counted among them a certain Alexandre Lacazette, as well as Clément Grenier, Enzo Reale, and two left-footed players, Yannis Tafer and Xavier Chavalerin. 'Griezmann came to train with us four or five times on Wednesday afternoons,' Chavalerin remembers. 'He was small and had great technique, but it was his haircut, mid-length and a bit like a cauliflower, that I remember the most.'

'What worked against him,' continues Duthéron 'was mainly that he didn't live in Lyon. It was impossible for him to travel 120 kilometres there and back every day. So he had to be provided with accommodation, a cost that the club was rarely prepared to bear at that age.' Nevertheless, Duthéron and Gérard Bonneau, OL's head of recruitment, went to Mâcon to have Antoine sign a non-solicitation agreement, according to Serge Rivera, former president of UF Mâconnais. 'But Alain Griezmann refused to sign it. I couldn't understand why,' says Rivera.

AS Saint-Étienne and AJ Auxerre were also keeping a watchful eye, but they didn't make Antoine an offer in the end. 'We liked him as a footballer but he was clearly lacking physically,' explains Vincent Cabin, at AJ Auxerre since 1999. Antoine was later summoned for a couple of trials with FC Metz. The recruiter Kodjo

Afiadegnigban still remembers everything about the episode: 'The decision was taken to have him sign with the club ... But shortly afterwards, and without any explanation, FC Metz went back on their decision.' When his father told him the news, Antoine burst into tears. 'Metz is the most painful memory,' he later told the media.

On May 2005, Antoine and his teammate Stevie Antunes where invited to take part with Montpellier Hérault SC in the international tournament for thirteen year olds at Saint-Germain-en-Laye. 'He had a good tournament, but we had already recruited for his position,' says Serge Delmas, the director of the Montpellier training centre. 'If we had seen Antoine in March or April, it would have been different, but he had turned up in May when the groups for the following season had been sewn up.'

The kid did not know it yet but that Camp des Loges tournament probably changed the course of his life.

When asked about his first meeting with Griezmann, Éric Olhats has always put it down to pure chance. According to his version, he had just come back from a trip to Argentina. Before returning home to Bayonne, he took advantage of landing in Paris to make a detour to the international tournament where he fell for the little blond boy. But according to Manu Christophe, the Montpellier recruiter, Éric Olhats went to Paris with one clear objective: to see Antoine at work. 'I was the one who told him about the player and that was well before … Some time later he ended up signing for Real Sociedad. Since then, Olhats has been very careful not to talk about how he discovered him.'

Antoine recalls, 'Someone slipped me a piece of paper. It was Éric Olhats, a French-speaking representative of Spanish side Real Sociedad. On the piece of paper he had written: "Don't open this until you get home!" Of course, I opened it two hours later. It said: "We would like you to have a week-long trial with us."'

Unsurprisingly, professional clubs were knocking on Paul Pogba's door after his performances in the U14 league with Torcy. 'The first time I saw him was in 2006. What struck me was the accuracy he already had in the long game and I immediately told Oualid about him,' Grégory Agelisas said during an interview with TF1.

At that time, Agelisas and Oualid Tanazefti were part of the Le Havre Athletic Club (HAC) recruitment team assembled by Franck Sale: 'They told me they had seen some great players, particularly a phenomenon called Paul Pogba. So I made the trip down. The first time I saw him play it wasn't with Torcy but in his home neighbourhood of La Renardière, with his friends. That might seem surprising but it was something that was quite common at the time. It allowed us to see players in a different context and it was often very revealing. I discovered a very confident lad that day, he was a leader and very charismatic.'

Olympique Lyonnais and AJ Auxerre had also

spotted the player, but the Normandy club convinced Yeo Moriba to allow her son to visit HAC for a few days' trial in early November 2006. 'Franck Sale and I managed to get him to sign because Auxerre and Lyon were both waiting in the wings,' Tanazefti told *Le Pays d'Auge* in 2016. The deal was done with a minimum of fuss in November 2006, when Paul signed a non-solicitation agreement.

Paul Pogba set his course towards Seine-Maritime to join HAC in 2007, just as he was enjoying his final year in the U15 age category. 'Paul would finish school every day at 3.30pm and had about 30 minutes to get to the academy by minibus, change and be on the pitch by 4pm. Training would last for two hours,' explains the former academy director, Alain Olio. 'He would then have to do his homework and tutoring. Dinner was served at 7pm, followed by free time with his instructors.' Weekends were devoted to competition, but the 'Parisians' had the right to special treatment: 'For us it was really important that they got to see their families. We set up a routine so they could go home one weekend out of every three.'

Mickaël Le Baillif was his coach: 'Paul came from an amateur club, and there were things that needed to be put in place … He was still playing a very pure and natural form of football. He had a tendency not to follow instructions.' During the 2007–08 season, Le Havre took a leading role in the U15 league. In a system with two defensive midfielders, 'Paul grew in strength over the course of the games. We finished second in the league behind PSG, but Paul played a prominent role and had been one of the best on the pitch.'

Twenty-eighth of October 2008. Stade Auguste-Delaune in Maison-Alfort, to the south-east of Paris. The France U16 team were preparing to play their first game in the Val-de-Marne tournament against Uruguay. Winning his third cap, Paul found himself in the midfield, charged with resisting the onslaught of the Celeste and supplying the two strikers. The plan worked well, as the defence held firm and Yaya Sanogo found two openings up front at the beginning of the second half. 'He certainly worked hard, but he always went too far. He thought he could manage everything himself.' This was the assessment of the first match provided by the manager, Guy Ferrier.

This analysis was similar to that of the coaches at Le Havre. 'The first months of the 2008–09 season weren't easy for him,' explains François Rodrigues. 'He had trouble focusing.' But there was someone in the stands who did not necessarily share this opinion. As soon as the final whistle had blown, this someone picked up his phone to talk to his superiors: 'I called Geoff Watson, head scout at the academy to tell him I'd just seen a player we should be very interested in ... The director of the academy, Jimmy Ryan, joined me for the next game to see the player for himself.'

This anecdote comes courtesy of David Friio, Manchester United's recruiter in France in early 2009.

'When I saw Paul that day I said to myself that he had the profile to play at United. Of course, with his lanky physique it was clear that he didn't find running easy because he was still growing. But he had exceptional touch. He gave himself time on the ball and shone because of that. From that game onwards, I began following him to see if my first impression had been right.'

A meeting in Manchester was set for mid-March, coinciding with the young international's sixteenth birthday. Fassou Antoine Pogba, Yeo Moriba, Paul's representative Gaël Mahé and David Friio went with Paul on this trip to the Theatre of Dreams. 'We took a detour through the city centre,' explains the former Manchester United recruiter. 'Then we went to the academy and bumped into the first team. We took a tour of the facilities, visited the stadium and went to Sir Alex Ferguson's office ... By the time we left the office, the kid had already made up his mind.'

Paul Pogba signed for Manchester United on 30 July 2009. When the news came out, those in charge at the Le Havre club made their anger clear in a statement that expressed their 'indignation regarding the dealings of Manchester United's directors' who had not respected the contract and offered 'very high sums of money to the parents ... with the aim of obtaining the transfer of their son to England.' In Manchester there was a different opinion: 'Quite simply because the non-solicitation agreement signed by Paul with Le Havre was only valid between French clubs,' explains Yves Martin, sports adviser. Moreover, 'if the directors at Le Havre had really wanted to protect him, they could have had him sign an elite contract, and then there would have been nothing more to say. But they didn't do that.'

According to leaks in the French media, Manchester United were reported to have offered €100,000 to both Paul's parents, as well as a house so his mother could come to live with him in Manchester. 'Not true,' according to David Friio. Yves Martin is more measured: 'There was a proper three-year plan for his football that allowed him to join the academy … But there were also a few things in return: the club found them an apartment and provided them with a driver. His mother also had to sign an employment contract and earn an income for looking after her son.'

On 7 October 2009, Manchester United emerged victorious from the wrangle with the Normandy club: 'Manchester United is pleased to confirm that the Football Association has been authorised by FIFA to register Paul Pogba as a Manchester United player with immediate effect,' the Red Devils proudly announced.

Reda Hammache was one of the first representatives of a professional club to fall for Kylian Mbappé. Aged 27, he was an instructor at US Saint-Denis and a recruiter for the Paris region on behalf of Stade Rennais. This second role took him to Bondy in February 2009: 'The pitch was as hard as cement that day but it didn't stop me from appreciating Kylian's talents. As he was playing two years above his age category, he was smaller and frailer, but he already looked great and had a natural elegance. Whenever he touched the ball, something always happened. I immediately saw that he was head and shoulders above the rest.'

In May 2009, the young winger was called up for a tournament in Giff-sur-Yvette, about twenty kilometres to the south-west of Paris. Kylian was included in the team entrusted to Reda Hammache. To get him to understand the importance of playing as a team, the young coach decided to move him to right-back for one game. 'He didn't stay in his position even for a second. He constantly came forward … I made him understand that, as an instructor, I couldn't afford to pick a player who didn't listen to me. So he was going to be a substitute for the next game.'

The little pearl of Bondy began the following match on the bench, sulking and pouting until his team won a free-kick in a good position just outside the penalty area. 'I called Kylian over and told him: "You're going on. This time I want you to play in an attacking position. Enjoy yourself, but first, take this free-kick for me." He ran off, took the time to place the ball, shot … and scored! He came to celebrate his goal with me by jumping into my arms. It sealed our friendship.'

Despite this positive experience, the Breton club failed to attract Kylian. Stade Malherbe Caen – a modest French first division club – spotted Kylian in September 2009. 'He's a future Ballon d'Or winner,' was how David Lasry, the eyes of the Normandy club in the Paris region, described his latest find. He came to see the player on several occasions and spoke with Wilfrid Mbappé about how the club did things.

In the meantime, Reda Hammache had left Stade Rennais to join Racing Club de Lens, so they too were on the lookout and the family eventually made the trip to Northern France in June 2010. PSG offered to take Kylian to a tournament in Spain, but he chose instead to answer the call from Caen to play in the Jean-Pingeon Challenge, where he would be voted player of the competition. Other French clubs joined the discussions and in the spring of 2011, Chelsea invited Kylian to spend a week at the Cobham training centre. It was a unique experience that would allow the little prodigy to discover a new mindset, meet Didier Drogba and, most importantly, pull on a Blues shirt for a friendly.

But Chelsea would not win the jackpot and Kylian's parents agreed to take more meetings with representatives from Lens and Caen in May 2011. A few weeks later, it was decided that Kylian would join the Caen Academy in two years' time, in August 2013, with a training-apprentice contract that would automatically lead to a professional deal. Caen would also have to pay a signing bonus set at €120,000 or €180,000 depending on the level of the first team at the time of Kylian's arrival.

While waiting to join the Caen academy at fifteen, he entered the National Football Institute in

Clairefontaine-en-Yvelines, about 50 kilometres to the south-west of Paris, in August 2015. Kylian passed the selection tests with flying colours and impressed his audience. 'I fell in love with the kid at first sight,' remembers Gérard Prêcheur, former director of the INF. 'As his grades were satisfactory, he was unsurprisingly one of the 22 players selected from among the 2,000 candidates. He would come to us on Sunday nights to train every day at Clairefontaine, while attending school with a tailored curriculum at the Collège Catherine de Vivonne in Rambouillet. On Friday nights, he would return to his family and play at his club during the weekend, above his age category.'

As the months went on, the agreement with Stade Malherbe Caen became more and more shaky. The Normandy club were in great difficulty on the footballing front and their budget had been cut. The little prodigy from Seine-Saint-Denis would again find himself at the top of many clubs' wish lists and Real Madrid called Wilfrid to invite his son for a week's trial. 'It fell right in the week of his birthday,' his parents told the local press. 'So, we didn't really go to Spain to find out more about his potential but to give him a treat.'

Kylian gave a blow-by-blow account of the trip, in December 2012, to a French weekly: 'The first day, we had seats to watch a Liga game against Espanyol. The next morning we went to the academy. Monsieur Zidane showed us around a bit, then I took part in my first training session … I also played in a match. On the fourth day, I saw the players. I had my photo taken with all of them!'

'Even today, people are still asking me why Kylian didn't go to Real,' reported Pierre Mbappé in an interview. 'It's simple. Because he was very young at the time and there was no guarantee it would work ... He would have had to have adapted to a new language, a new club and it would have involved a categorical change of life for the entire family. There was plenty of discussion and a choice was made.' Real Madrid, Manchester City, Girondins de Bordeaux and Paris Saint-Germain were all pipped at the post by a second division club, AS Monaco. In the spring of 2013, the club from the principality had been bought by the Russian billionaire Dmitry Rybolovlev and Reda Hammache had joined their recruitment team led by Souleymane Camara: 'I ended up convincing Wilfrid and Fayza to meet my boss Souleymane Camara and the director of the academy Frédéric Barilaro. It clicked immediately as they knew how to talk to parents and presented a plan that was consistent with Kylian's ambitions.' On 3 July 2013, after four years of negotiations, Kylian Mbappé officially signed a three-year apprentice contract with a signing bonus above €400,000, according to some sources.

Chapter 5

Academy

Antoine Griezmann arrived at the Zubieta complex in San Sebastián in the late spring of 2005. He trained three or four times with the fourteen year olds, who were under Íñigo Cortés. 'I said he was an interesting kid,' comments Cortés, 'even if he was small and very skinny, and that this was really obvious when he went up against someone bigger than him. In the end it was decided that Antoine would come back.'

Antoine began his adventure with Real Sociedad on 16 August 2005, after the summer holidays. He signed for one year, an agreement that could be terminated after three months if the boy did not settle into his new life. Real agreed to pay his expenses, plus a monthly plane ticket so his parents could come and visit. He would not live at the club's boarding school but with Éric Olhats, who offered to take him into his home in Bayonne.

Olhats played the role of father, mother, spiritual adviser, confidant and chauffeur, driving him backwards and forwards between his home and Zubieta. '[Éric's] a good person,' explains Alex Ruiz, a French goalkeeper who lived for almost three years with Antoine in the scout's home, 'someone very endearing, always ready to listen, but very demanding with us, even when it came to school – one thing that certainly wasn't a passion for me or Antoine.'

Antoine's first coach was Luki Iriarte, with whom he spent two seasons: 2005–06 and 2006–07. Iriarte recalls: 'Back then he was neither strong nor did he have pace. He was small, skinny and fragile, but he made up for his physical weaknesses with his talent. … He had the technique and he knew where the ball was going half a second before the others. He knew how to gain an advantage with his first touch.'

Despite his obvious talent, at that time he was often relegated to the bench. 'He wasn't imposing but he knew exactly where he wanted to go. He wanted to play in the first division. It was an objective he had obviously set himself,' continues Ruiz. However, Antoine still had to wait for another two years before finally making a breakthrough at the San Sebastián club.

Oualid Tanazefti, Paul Pogba's representative, moved to Manchester; Yeo, Paul's mother, also joined him, but integrating into a different world, a more physical kind of football and a place where everyone speaks another language came at a price. 'His English wasn't the best at first, but he was a chatty, confident guy and obviously he was confident in his football too. He believed in his ability and he believed in himself,' John Cofie, one of his teammates, would tell Sky Sports years later.

Pogba played his first match with Paul McGuinness's Young Reds on 10 October 2009: 'The first time I saw him, all six foot three of him, I thought, "Wow, he looks the part." He had a great smile and long levers. Normally at that age, boys are growing and they lack coordination, but he had it.'

There were plenty of good players in that group. Ravel Morrison, born and brought up in Wythenshawe, was considered the brightest hope of the 1993 squad. 'Every day between Ravel and Paul was a challenge,' remembers McGuinness. 'They never stopped coming up with new tricks in training. They had an outlet for their need to overdo things in the playground session, where the kids are free to play however they want, like in street football.' That year, the U18s qualified for the play-off semi-final of the Premier League Academy. On 7 May 2010, they were eliminated by Arsenal on penalties: 3–5 after a 1–1 draw.

'The 2010–11 season was crazy,' remembers McGuinness. 'A fantastic experience for the boys who grew up together and gained in confidence game after game.' In the FA Youth Cup, United knocked out Portsmouth, West Ham, Newcastle, Liverpool and Chelsea to reach the final of the tournament. On Monday 23 May 2011, the day after the big boys had won the Premier League, the youngsters in red beat Sheffield United 4–1 in the return leg to win the cup.

It was the Red Devils' tenth since the competition had begun in 1953. No English club had won more. The boys celebrated by lifting the cup under the watchful eye of Sir Alex and the 23,000 fans in attendance. There was no doubt they made a great team!

Things took a turn during the 2011–12 season and it all began on 20 September 2011. After 45 minutes at Elland Road against Leeds United in the third round of the Carling Cup, United were 3–0 up. It was as a substitute for Ryan Giggs that, at the beginning of the second half, Paul Pogba made his debut with the big boys. He did not hold back in tackles, picked up the ball, was on the receiving end of two bad fouls, won a free-kick, tried a couple of long-range shots and played until the end of the game. The overall verdict was positive, but in the months to come he only made it onto the pitch twice, as a substitute in Carling Cup matches on both occasions.

On Saturday 31 December 2011, Blackburn Rovers, who were bottom of the Premier League, paid a visit to Old Trafford. 'Paul Scholes had retired. Darren Fletcher was injured. There was no one left to play in midfield. I was training and the coach never stopped telling me "You're this far." And I didn't understand. This far from what? From having some playing time? From getting on the field?' Pogba told Canal+ in 2014. 'I didn't get on the field for the whole game. I lost the relationship I had with the manager and I was really disappointed.'

When, at the beginning of January, he heard that Scholes had agreed to come out of retirement, Paul thought his chances had been reduced even further. His long-awaited Premier League debut eventually came on 31 January 2012 in a home game against Stoke, but it only lasted a handful of minutes. His three-year contract expired in 2012; he had the option of renewing it for a further year, but, at the behest of Oualid Tanazefti, Carmine 'Mino' Raiola, the Dutch–Italian agent responsible for both Balotelli and Ibrahimović, got involved.

'There are one or two football agents I simply do not like, and Mino Raiola is one of them,' Alex Ferguson would say in his latest book, *Leading*. Yeo Moriba told *AFP*, 'Ferguson punished him because of that and wouldn't let him play ... He even ended up crying in the manager's office because of how he had been treated.' There was no doubt that the boy was unhappy; Paul swore he loved Manchester and United, but Bayern Munich, Real Madrid and PSG, according to Oualid Tanazefti in 2016, were all courting him.

There were others as well: Raiola was knocking on the doors of clubs in Italy. 'Don't go to Italy, there's racism there,' Ferguson is said to have told him to put him off. Pogba was unsure, thinking it would be a backward step, but eventually signed for Juventus for next to nothing. It was the end, or at least for the time being, of Paul's love story with United.

*

During his first season at Monaco, Kylian was housed alongside his teammates underneath the arches of the Stade Louis II, where about twenty rooms are made available to young recruits. Every morning, they would climb into a minibus headed for La Turbie, a small French town about ten kilometres from the principality, to spend the day at the academy. The morning was dedicated to schoolwork, where Year 11 classes were given on site. In the middle of the afternoon, it was time for training, on a magnificent artificial pitch looking out over the Mediterranean.

For his first games in the U17 National League, Kylian was rarely in the starting eleven but came on intermittently at the end of a few matches. On 8 September 2013, Bruno Irlès, his coach, decided to send his young recruit to the amateur section to strengthen the team playing in the U17 Division d'Honneur. It would turn out to be the first source of conflict. 'It was noted in the match report that he had made a hand gesture towards his coach, who had asked him to track back and defend,' detailed Irlès. 'More surprisingly, it wasn't him who was summoned the following week, it was me! Frédéric Barilaro and Souleymane Camara had received a phone call from Kylian's parents, who couldn't understand why I'd sent their son to play in the Division d'Honneur. The result was that they told me not to make him play at that level again.'

Wilfrid Mbappé had taken a year's sabbatical to move

into an apartment close to the training centre and was frankly not happy. According to Irlès, 'I was criticised for Kylian's lack of playing time. I replied that I'd been banned from making him play with the amateurs and that he didn't have the right mindset yet to be in the starting eleven for the U17 National League. They also told me it was my fault that the boy was unhappy, but that wasn't true ... Lastly, they talked to me about harassment during the training sessions. My response was that an instructor has to be able to shake up a player sometimes when he's not listening to instructions.'

Bruno Irlès left AS Monaco to prepare for his qualification as a professional coach and Kylian would eventually finish his first season in the France U17 league with 1,175 minutes spent on the pitch, half the possible playing time. Irlès would also come across some statistics in the notes he wrote at the time: five goals scored, including two against Nîmes, three assists and ... two direct errors that resulted in a goal. 'Yep, I make a note of what's bad as well as what's good. You don't get the chance to go back and do it over!'

Kylian's second year would be much more enjoyable: 'He had got used to how the training centre worked and was fully integrated,' explains the former head of recruitment Souleymane Camara. 'With a team of instructors who were much more in line with his way of thinking, he felt freer and soon regained his confidence. And when Kylian is happy, that's often when he does exceptional things.' During the second half of the season, he would barely leave Frédéric Barilaro's U19 squad, scoring a total of eight goals.

The 2015–16 season would be a record breaker. On 3 October, after only seven U19 league games, Kylian had already scored ten goals and provided two assists. 'I saw a boy who was completely transformed,' says Marc Westerloppe, who had been working at PSG for more than two years by then. 'He was ready for the top level. He'd grown and his muscles were beginning to form. There was a feeling that something would happen once he'd gained a few kilos.' In mid-October, the sixteen-year-old kid made his debut with the reserve team in the CFA league, France's fourth division.

In mid-November, during an international break, Mbappé joined the pro squad managed by Leonardo Jardim. And that was where he stayed. He would rejoin the U19 team only for the last rounds of the French U19 cup. On Saturday 21 May 2016 at the Stade de France, Kylian achieved the Holy Grail for any player from an academy by winning the Coupe Gambardella in a final against Racing Club de Lens during which he reached another level. 'Things were always easy with Kylian,' remembered Cardona in 2017; he would have a front row seat in the second half to see the number 10 score two goals at the Stade de France for the first time. 'I don't know if I'll ever get to play with him again, but he's probably the person I've had the best understanding with on a football pitch.'

Chapter 6

The breakthrough

Four lines in the sports section on 30 July 2009. 'Antoine Griezmann', wrote *El Diario Vasco*, 'trained with the first team yesterday. Martín Lasarte selected the Burgundian striker, who plays on the left wing, to train with the professional squad for the first time. Griezmann, eighteen, joined the reserve Txuri Urdin this summer after an impressive season with the youth teams.'

'The situation was complicated and difficult. Real had been vegetating in the second division for two years,' recalls Lasarte. 'We had a squad of 21 or 22 players and the only position that still needed to be filled was that of understudy on the left wing. I asked those in charge of the training academy to send me a player who fitted that profile and they sent me a young French player who, to be frank, I hadn't heard of.'

First of August 2009, the Txerloia ground in Azkoitia. The first pre-season game was played against CD Anaitasuna, a team from Spanish football's sixth division. After the first half, Real Sociedad were leading 3–0. As expected, at the beginning of the second half,

Lasarte kicked off with an eleven composed primarily of young players. Among them, for his first match with the first team, was Antoine Griezmann. Wearing a red shirt and in torrential rain, he tried to score every time he got the ball, managed to nutmeg an opponent by the corner post and scored two goals with good left-footed strikes.

On 5 August, Lasarte brought him on for the second half against the third division team FC Barakaldo and Griezmann scored twice again. The local media were in a frenzy. Faced with so much enthusiasm, and not wanting everyone to get carried away, Real Sociedad called time. He would not return to the pitch until 12 August, in Ipurua, against Eibar. Once again, he caused a sensation with a stunning goal that gave the Txuri Urdin the victory. Antoine was the revelation of the summer.

Martín Lasarte decided to give him the chance to christen his new season's shirt on 2 September 2009 at the Anoeta, against Rayo Vallecano in the Copa del Rey. Just ten minutes in a 2–0 loss.

On 6 September 2009, they played host to Murcia at the Anoeta for the second match of the league season. Coming off the bench in the 73rd minute, Griezmann made his league debut at eighteen years, five months and sixteen days. In a very dull match that ended in a 0–0 draw, the youngster had not been at his best but was still on the receiving end of lengthy applause from the Basque supporters.

On 27 September 2009, for the fifth match of

the season against Huesca at the Anoeta, Antoine Griezmann took Jonathan Estrada's place on the left wing in the starting eleven for the first time. In the 38th minute, Antoine found himself on the end of a good ball during an attack. He did not hesitate even for a second: he shifted into gear and let rip with his right foot from the edge of the area, sending a mid-height shot into the back of Miguel's net. Grizi ran towards the terraces with open arms, grasped his shirt and kissed the blue and white shield.

The following day, *AS* was sure that 'the Anoeta has witnessed the birth of a new star, named Antoine Griezmann.'

On 3 August 2012 at the Juventus headquarters on Corso Galileo Ferraris, Paul Pogba signed a contract that would tie him to the Vecchia Signora for four years (with a salary just short of €1.5 million): 'I'm very happy with this new path I'm about to take. I hope to have a great season. In Manchester, I learned from champions such as Scholes, Rio Ferdinand and Rooney. I'm sure it'll be the same at Juve with Pirlo.'

Of course, Andrea Pirlo was the first to realise that the boy was strong and skinny but with legs that could get everywhere. 'I remember on Pogba's first day of training we burst out laughing. We couldn't believe that a club as important as Manchester United would allow such a talented young player to leave on a free transfer,' remembers the Italian.

The boy made his Serie A debut on 22 September 2012 in a home game against Chievo. At age nineteen, he did not have Pirlo's vision of the game, but he knew what to do with the ball at his feet, was a good sweeper and did not turn his nose up at moving forward and trying to score, so the experiment worked. Juve registered their fourth win in a row in as many league games and Paul was rated satisfactory by the press.

His first goal with the Bianconeri came in a top-of-the-table clash against Napoli on 20 October. Paul substituted Vidal in the 30th minute of the second half and, seven minutes later, Giovinco tried a shot from outside the area that came back off Paolo Cannavaro; the loose ball fell for Pogba, who, without hesitation, connected with it perfectly and fired it into the lower left corner of De Sanctis' net. It was the match-winning goal! Paul ran towards the stand where his cousins were watching, proud of having scored in front of them. After the game, which took Juve to the top of the table, Paul played around with French and English as he talked about his goal: 'I gave it a try and it went well. But it's just one goal, one football match, and I won't let it go to my head.'

The French player was eventually called up with increasing regularity, but life in black and white was not always a bed of roses. Tardiness at training sessions was inexcusable. Paul was late on 9 November and, as a result, was not picked for the away match against Pescara the following day. 'I'm really sorry about it. And of course I'd like to apologise,' he said in a long interview with *Tuttosport*. After the excuses came the chatting. Paul talked about Juve, where, unlike at United, he said he felt appreciated: 'The players believe in me, the manager believes in me, I have the opportunity to play.' Among his teammates, Buffon and Marchisio were the ones who surprised him most and then there was Pirlo: 'impressive, incredible, it's amazing to play alongside him.' What about Conte? 'He's more serious than Ferguson in training. He requires maximum focus. I like him because he's a winner.'

On 19 January 2013, under a grey Torinese sky that threatened snow, the Bianconeri were playing the blue shirts of Udinese at the Juventus Stadium. It was the 41st minute and the score was locked at 0–0. The young French player, sporting a yellow Mohican, took a seemingly innocuous ball out of the air outside the area, 35 yards from the opposition's goal. He fired a curving shot violently with the outside of his right foot. Some claimed it even came close to reaching 100 kilometres per hour! The meteorite grazed the crossbar and hit the back of the net. In 66th minute, he scored again, with a similar missile. It was the birth of PogBOOM!

A catapult from distance was to become Pogba's trademark. Whenever he got anywhere near the outside of the box, the packed J-Stadium would shout: 'Shoot, shoot, shoooooot!!!' It had not taken Paul many games to become an idol.

Pogba, now twenty, won his first *scudetto* with Juventus

on 5 May with a 1–0 victory in Palermo. He finished with 37 appearances (league and cup) and five goals. He was a revelation to everyone, the surprise of the Serie A season.

On 2 December 2015, Mbappé's big moment finally arrived: Kylian took his first steps in Ligue 1 in the 1–1 draw against Stade Malherbe Caen, replacing Portuguese defender Fábio Coentrão in the 88th minute. At the age of sixteen years, eleven months and twelve days, he became the youngest player for his club to play for the first team and wiped Thierry Henry from the record books for the first time.

On 20 February 2016, during his ninth appearance for the first team, Kylian found his way to goal for the first time, scoring against Troyes to make it 3–1 in injury time. About ten minutes after coming on, he took advantage of a good pick-up by Helder Costa and a return pass from the Portuguese midfielder to surge into the area, before striking a low shot with his left foot and wrong-footing the keeper. At seventeen years and two months, Kylian had just become the youngest professional goal scorer in the history of AS Monaco.

His three-year training-apprentice contract would expire at the end of June 2016 and, just four months before this deadline, AS Monaco had still not 'locked in' its player by formalising his first professional contract. Several meetings took place in Paris between the player's family and PSG's director of football at the time, Olivier Létang, who was already envisaging a five-year plan. At the same time, Arsenal entered the fray and Arsène Wenger himself made the trip to try to convince Kylian's family.

A few days after his first start in Ligue 1 (28 February at the Stade de la Beaujoire in Nantes), Monaco's sporting director, Luis Campos, intervened: 'I saw Kylian's mother at training and spent 40 minutes with her and explained that at PSG or Arsenal, he would arrive in a dressing room made up of big personalities and egos and no one would speak to him. He needed to wait a bit.' On 6 March 2016, AS Monaco formalised the signing of Kylian Mbappé's first professional contract. The three-year agreement was accompanied by a signing bonus of €3 million for the player and a starting salary of €85,000, which would be re-evaluated over the next two years. It was a vote of confidence that Mbappé would succeed in repaying magnificently during the last few months of the season.

In the absence of Falcao, Vágner Love and Valère Germain, Kylian was in the starting eleven for the kick-off to the Ligue 1 season on Friday 12 August 2016 at the Stade Louis II against Guingamp. Unfortunately, he was knocked out in the 40th minute after a clash of heads with the defender Christophe Kerbrat and rushed to hospital with a concussion.

Kylian returned to the pitch on 10 September for a CFA league game with the reserve team and imagined he would rejoin the pros the following week for the Champions League game against Tottenham. But, to the amazement of those close to Kylian, his name did not appear on the team sheet for the highly anticipated trip to White Hart Lane. According to some sources, Kylian burst into tears when it was announced he would not be playing and even disappeared for several hours.

Mbappé did not play at all against Rennes, Nice or Angers. On 13 October 2016, Wilfrid Mbappé revealed his discontent in an interview given to *L'Equipe*: 'This situation is not making Kylian happy and you can see it on his face during the week. He needs to be playing at his age so we'll have to think hard about the winter transfer window.'

Kylian was therefore well aware of the stakes when he was told he had been picked for his second start in the French league a few hours before kick-off for the game against Montpellier. He didn't disappoint. Two goals, two assists and 6–2 at the end, a fabulous break-through for Mbappé.

This would be followed by a resounding end to the year. Before the Christmas break, he racked up four more league starts, one goal and two assists. His star just kept rising. On 14 December, for his club's entry into the League Cup competition, he put on a show against Stade Rennais in the last sixteen. He scored his first goal in the eleventh minute with a burst of speed down the left wing before opening up his right foot perfectly. In the twentieth minute, he helped in a cross deflected by Nabil Dirar at the far post, then distinguished himself for one last time in the 62nd minute on the end of an assist from João Moutinho that he converted with his left foot. At just seventeen years, eleven months and 24 days, this time Kylian had become the youngest ever player to score a hat-trick in a Monaco shirt.

Chapter 7

On top

'This is a once-in-a-lifetime moment. We should enjoy every second.' Soaked to the skin, exhausted, with his white t-shirt drenched in water and the flag of the Basque Country across his shoulders, Antoine stops in front of a pack of journalists. The young man's joy flows out of him. When asked by a reporter if he would like 'to spend the rest of his life in the first division,' he says 'Yes!' before disappearing down the dressing room tunnel.

Real Sociedad had just officially confirmed promotion to La Liga at the end of the penultimate match of the league season with a 2–0 win over Celta Vigo. San Sebastián was happy again and Griezmann had plenty to do with that. With his carefree attitude and youth, he had given the whole city its smile back. Everyone still remembers 9 January 2010. In the nineteenth match of the league season, Real Sociedad were at home to Cádiz. In the 90th minute, the Txuri Urdin were leading 3–1 when suddenly, Antoine picked up the ball in the midfield, sped down the right wing, broke into the box and fired a shot in over Kiko Casilla's head. To celebrate his fifth goal in the second division, he dived into a mountain of snow piled up at the edge of the pitch as if he were jumping into a swimming pool. 'He wanted to do something funny,' remembers Lasarte, with a smile, 'but I think he hurt himself because the snow was really hard, almost frozen solid.'

Antoine Griezmann had become the darling of the supporters and they had nicknamed him 'Superantoine', 'Fabuloso', 'El Mago' (The Magician) or 'El ángel caído del cielo' (The Angel Fallen from the Sky). He moved from Bayonne to San Sebastián, releasing himself from Éric Olhats's protection, and went to live with Carlos Bueno before renting with Emilio Nsue, who was two years older and shared his passion for the PlayStation, dancing and having fun.

The 2010–11 season started on 29 August. Real faced Villareal at the Anoeta and Grizi was on the substitutes' bench. This was not a managerial whim, the Frenchman was simply lacking in fitness. He came on for Paco Sutil in the 61st minute. His debut in the Spanish first division was something that had motivated him since his arrival at the Zubieta. Real Sociedad's big return to La Liga went very well indeed. They beat the 'Yellow Submarine' 1–0, making the dreams of the 24,865 spectators in the Anoeta come true.

Antoine had to be content with coming on towards the end of the next few games, a series of disappointments. On 25 October, against Deportivo de

La Coruña, the club could finally take some heart from a win marked by Antoine's first goal in La Liga and an unforgettable celebration. In the 70th minute, Xabi Prieto swapped places with Martínez and moved to the right, before measuring a cross right into the middle of the box. Antoine jumped up, found himself in space in front of a defender and his teammate Llorente and fired the ball into the back of the net. He ran to the corner post, jumped over the advertising hoardings, crossed the athletics track and got into the driving seat of the Opel parked in the area reserved for Real's sponsors. Pretending to drive off, he was joined by his acolytes Prieto, Gorka Elustondo and Alberto De La Bella.

'I'm the happiest kid in the world!' Antoine confessed in the post-match interview. 'I'd been preparing that celebration for a while.' The quirky celebration earned him a yellow card but he didn't care. He knew that Burger King had launched a competition to reward the most original celebration that season. 'We talked about it,' Antoine admitted, 'and we thought we could win. I hope we'll have other opportunities to surprise people.'

Amid transfer rumours and otherwise nondescript performances loomed the Basque derby against Athletic Bilbao, the first after three years of waiting. On 5 December 2010, the Blue-and-Whites beat the Leones 2–0 with surprising ease thanks to a penalty converted by Prieto and an own goal from San José. Griezmann came very close to scoring the goal of the game: after pinching the ball out of Iraizoz's hands with his head, he saw his shot come back off the post as the goal gaped.

The success of the derby was followed by four consecutive defeats. The Txuri Urdin escaped relegation at the very last minute thanks to wins at home against Sporting Gijon, Zaragoza, Barcelona and a mutually beneficial draw with Getafe on the final day of the league season. Antoine Griezmann had played 37 matches in La Liga and two in the Copa del Rey, with a total of seven goals. Despite having achieved this objective and with a year still to run on his contract, it was not enough to guarantee Martín Lasarte his place in the dugout next season. On 25 May, four days after the end of the season, the Uruguayan was pushed out in favour of Philippe Montanier.

On 4 August 2011, from Colombia, where he was playing for France U19, Griezmann issued a statement through the newspaper *L'Équipe* that he wanted to leave Real Sociedad: 'I've made my decision. I want to go to Atlético Madrid because they compete regularly for European trophies.' Miguel Ángel Gil Marín, the Atlético administrator, had had the French player in his sights for a long time as the ideal replacement for Sergio Agüero, who had gone to Manchester City. But he was not the only one targeting Real's number 7, as there were rumours of interest from Pep Guardiola and Barça.

The story was not a new one and on 4 October, another scandal broke out, in the calm of Clairefontaine, where the French U20 team were preparing for two Euro 2013 qualifying matches. When Alban Lagoutte from *Football.fr* asked him 'Will you have to leave Real Sociedad next summer for a bigger club?' Antoine replied: 'I hope to be able to do that next summer, yes. I'm currently in discussions with my president about my release clause.'

Griezmann's response provoked Jokin Aperribay's anger in the pages of *Marca*: 'What Griezmann has to do is find his best level, express himself on the pitch and score goals. I haven't discussed a lowering of his release clause with him. That's not true … His agent did come to the club three times but we told him that Antoine's contract runs until 2015.'

Alain Griezmann responded to the president's statements in an interview with the *Mundo Deportivo*. He did not justify his son's comments but rather believed Antoine had made a mistake, and that he had been taken for a ride by certain journalists who knew how to get a twenty-year-old kid to say whatever they wanted. 'He's been living away from the family home since he was fourteen. When Éric Olhats stopped being his confidant he began relying on Martín Lasarte. Now, from one day to the next, he's found himself alone.' But badly advised and influenced by his agent, John Williams, he added.

Williams' contract with the player came to an end

on 30 October 2011. It was said that he had pressurised Antoine over a transfer to Atlético Madrid so he could take a substantial cut with him when he left. No doubts were cast on the young Antoine, a victim of his inexperience. Montanier accepted his apology and hoped he would now be able to focus properly on his football. Between late 2011 and early 2012, Griezmann reemerged. On 14 January, against Valencia in Mestalla, Antoine scored again, his second league goal and his third of the season, securing all three points for his team. 'Antoine showed he was mentally tough,' remembers Philippe Montanier. He ended the 2011–12 season with seven goals in 35 league matches and one goal in three Copa del Rey games. One more goal than the previous two years. Real, on 47 points, ended the season in twelfth place.

Speculation about Antoine's future resurfaced during the summer transfer window. But this time, Antoine did not let the journalists get one over on him when they asked if he was planning to leave Real. He replied with a frank and direct 'No!'

On 30 September 2012, between two disappointments at Levante and Betis, the Anoeta played host to a Basque derby that was more hotly anticipated than usual due to the interest from Marcelo Bielsa's Athletic Bilbao in Griezmann the previous June. Antoine opened the scoring in the 62nd minute before Carlos Vela increased the lead from the penalty spot three minutes later. The game finished 2–0 and there was no doubt that the most pragmatic team had won. Unfortunately, as in the previous season, derby success was followed by two defeats at the Anoeta against Atlético Madrid and Espanyol.

Griezmann once again found the back of the net at Real Zaragoza's Romareda stadium on February, after a long wait. He opened the scoring and his team won 2–1. It was the turning point in his season and saw Real Sociedad begin their climb back up the table. He equalised at the San Mamés during the second derby of the season, won 3–1 by Real, scored twice in a 4–1 win over Valladolid and again in the 4–2 victory over Malaga. To top this off, he scored the only goal of the game against Deportivo de La Coruna at the Riazor on the final day of the Spanish league season. The goal saw Real clinch fourth place in the table and secure a Champions League spot. After a ten-year wait, the Txuri Urdin were back in Europe!

The follow-up would be more painful. After a strong performance against Olympique Lyonnais in the preliminary round, five defeats and a single but prestigious 0–0 draw at home to Manchester United earned the Txuri Urdin a last place finish in Group A behind the Red Devils, Bayer Leverkusen and Shakhtar Donetsk. Like his team, Antoine had nothing to celebrate, with no goals or assists in six starts.

Philippe Montanier had left the club on 4 June 2013 and had been replaced by Jagoba Arrasate, a modest

ex-player propelled to the head of the team at 35 years
of age. By 15 December, Antoine had already scored
ten league goals in the new season, equalling his record
for the entire 2012–13 season and becoming the best
French goalscorer in Europe in 2013. This maturity was
also owed to his girlfriend, Erika. 'She helped him focus
on football, on his career and on having the lifestyle of
a professional player,' explained Miguel González, a
journalist for the *Diario Vasco*. Erika Choperena, originally from Vera de Bidasoa in Navarre, is a teaching grad-
uate with a passion for fashion; she is elegant, quiet and
extremely discreet. She met Antoine in San Sebastián
in 2011 and it took almost a year for him to win her
over. When they decided to move in together, the daily
life of Real's number 7 gradually began to change. The
boy now preferred staying at home with Erika, going
to the beach, out for dinner or to the Donostia Arena
to watch Gipuzkoa Basketball Club matches with her
and his friends.

On 26 January 2014, against Elche at the Anoeta,
the number 7 was at it again. In the second minute,
on the end of a deep ball from Carlos Vela, he made
for the goal and threw a shot up over the opposing
keeper. Then, in the eleventh minute, a cross from Xabi
Prieto found its target as Antoine jumped to connect
with the ball and score. After Vela's goal to make it 3–0,
he got his hat-trick, the only one he would score for
Real. Griezmann pounced on a fumbled cross to volley
the ball into the back of the net, sealing the 4–0 win. It

was a shame that the first goal was eventually attributed to Damián Suárez, who, in a desperate attempt to clear the ball, had pushed it into the back of his own net. One goal fewer, making it 'only' fourteen goals for the French player, to which another was added during the 3–1 win inflicted, to general surprise, by Real Sociedad on Barça at home.

It was a response, or rather revenge for the Copa del Rey elimination eleven days earlier. On 12 February, during the return semi-final against the Blaugrana, Antoine managed to equalise after an early goal from Messi. The final score was 1–1 but Barça's 2–0 victory in the first leg, at Camp Nou, sent the Catalans into the final.

Between 23 February and the end of the La Liga season, Antoine Griezmann scored just once, taking his total to twenty goals across all competitions, in addition to three assists. Thanks to Antoine's goal drought and the lack of motivation of his teammates, Real had plunged from fifth to seventh in the end of season table, a position that would see them fail to qualify for their beloved Champions League.

The 112th Italian football league season began on 24 August 2013. Antonio Conte admitted that Pogba was 'growing, it will be hard to keep him on the bench.' He was no longer just a powerful midfielder with pace but he now had the numbers to be a starting eleven player in his own right, as well as Pirlo's deputy. When the Bianconero veteran was not available it was up to the twenty-year-old French player to orchestrate the Old Lady's midfield.

Juventus finished their Champions League group stage behind Real Madrid and Galatasaray. They could console themselves with a third place finish that meant the knock-out phase of the UEFA Europa League, where Paul scored his first goal in European competition on 20 February 2014 against Trabzonspor, in Turin. It was his seventh goal across all league and cup competitions. But on 1 May 2014, under violent rain at the Juventus Stadium, the Bianconeri could only manage a 0–0 draw in the second leg of their UEFA Cup semi-final against Benfica. The Portuguese team had won 2–1 in the first leg and closed the door on the match in Turin.

At least the domestic league could be counted on to raise Bianconero morale. Three days after the European debacle, on 4 May, Roma were taken apart at home by Catania (1–4), making Juventus champions for the third successive time. They finished the season with a record 102 points. They had won 33 matches of 38 played, with the best attack and the best defence in Serie A. The Golden Boy had the highest number of appearances (36 in the league, 51 in total) and had scored nine goals across all competitions.

Antonio Conte, the manager who had taken Juve to the *scudetto* for three years in a row, left on 15 July

2014, following differences of opinion over the transfer market and a decline in motivation. His place on the Juve bench was taken by Massimo Allegri, the former AC Milan manager. On 24 October, Beppe Marotta, the CEO, chose the Juventus shareholders' meeting to officially confirm Paul's marriage to the Turin club until 2019. The Golden Boy would see his salary triple to €4.5 million.

On 18 March 2015, a magical night in Dortmund that saw Juventus admitted to the last eight of European football, there was only bitterness and anger for Pogba. His match against Borussia would last only 26 minutes. A clash with Sokratis Papastathopoulos, the BVB 09 Greek defender, left him on the ground clutching his right thigh. Tests the following day revealed the worst: a second-degree lesion of the myotendinous junction of the right bicep's femoris muscle. Two months out. Until that night, he was significantly improving his record as a professional. One goal in the Champions League, one in the Coppa Italia and six in the domestic league.

With Paul still in the stands, the Bianconeri won 1–0 and secured the 31st league title in their history, the fourth in a row, with a 1–0 victory against Sampdoria in Genoa (2 May). Three days later, Real Madrid would be paying a visit to the Juventus Stadium for the first leg of the Champions League semi-final, and Alvaro Morata and Carlos Tevez would keep the dream alive (2–1). Paul, at last, was present for the return game eight days later. In the first twenty minutes, Bale, Benzema and

Ronaldo tried their best from all over the pitch, but Juve held firm. Then Chiellini brought James Rodriguez down in the box and the Swedish referee, Jonas Eriksson, blew for a penalty. Gigi Buffon failed to pull off a miracle when faced with Cristiano Ronaldo's crisp right-footed shot down the middle. One–nil to Madrid. The Merengues persisted and besieged Buffon, but then Morata scored the goal that saw Juventus qualify: a free-kick by Pirlo from the right, a tangle in the box and a punch from Casillas that cleared the ball. Vidal tried to put it back in; Pogba grazed it with his head and Morata came in like a train, controlled it with his chest and unleashed a left-footed shot. One–one and a ticket to the Champions League final against Barcelona.

Juve would win the double by beating Lazio 2–1 after 120 minutes in the Coppa Italia final. What happened during the Champions League final is now well known. With goals from Ivan Rakitić, Luis Suárez and Neymar, Juve lost their sixth final in eight attempts. Many blamed the penalty that never was, when Dani Alves held Pogba back inside the box right before half-time with the score line at 1–1. A few days later, the French player confessed to the microphones of Canal+: 'We were convinced we could go on to win. It hurts to lose. There was also a foul on me that should have been a penalty, but the referee didn't see it ... Congratulations to Barcelona, who deserved to lift the cup ... I hope to be able to lift it one day.'

*

Juve did not get their first win until the fourth game of the 2015–16 season, away from home against Genoa on 20 September: 2–0, with a Pogba penalty in the 60th minute. But it was a flash in the pan. On 28 October, a 1–0 loss to Sassuolo sent Allegri and Co. properly into crisis. Fans, directors and pundits alike were all asking what had happened to the player who used to do everything: defend, attack, score, win tackles and provide assists. He was nowhere to be seen on the pitch, a missing pawn on the black and white chessboard.

But from 31 October 2015, Juventus went on a streak of 24 wins and a single defeat. By December, they had qualified for the last sixteen of the Champions League and were back in the race for the *scudetto*. Paul, the boy who had been taught while in Turin to rest in order to play his best, to work hard, to eat well, to eat pasta, pasta and more pasta, was smiling again.

Just as he was on 20 December 2015, when he unveiled his Dab to the world. Juve were 2–1 up away at Carpi thanks to two goals from Mandžukić. As the second half was getting under way, Marchisio launched a long ball, an assist for Pogba who, finding himself alone in the box, controlled it with his chest and predicted that Belec, the Carpi keeper, would come off his line. Goal! He ran to the touchline, dropped his head, stuck out an arm and folded the other one to his chest. It was pure geometry. What kind of a way was that to celebrate a goal?

Paul, who loves everything American and the NBA in particular, had imported the celebration. He performed it with his new partner in crime Paulo Dybala and involved the Juventus dressing room and directors, even Pavel Nedved and Andrea Agnelli, the president of Juve, for an Instagram post on 11 January 2016 during the Ballon d'Or gala.

On 16 March 2016, Juventus faced Bayern Munich in the return leg of the first knock-out stage of the Champions League. Paul had missed the first leg on 23 February in Italy; it had ended in a draw (2–2). Thanks to Robert Lewandowski in the 73rd minute and Thomas Müller in injury time, Bayern wrestled back a 2–2 draw that meant parity across both legs. Despite what may well have been one of his busiest matches of the Champions League season, Paul was powerless in the 108th and 110th minutes; buoyed by their fans, the German champions pulled away with goals from Thiago Alcantara and Kingsley Coman.

La Pioche went out with a bang during the final games of the Italian season, with three goals and seven assists in the last nine games. In 2016, he was undefeated in Serie A and strung together an incredible series of 26 undefeated league games, including 25 victories, between 31 October 2015 and 14 May 2016. Juventus secured their 32nd *scudetto* ahead of Napoli and Paul finished his fourth season top of the class with eight goals in Serie A (ten across all competitions) and provided the most assists in the league (thirteen). As everything continued to go right for him, on 21 May 2016, the Bianconeri won the Coppa Italia to secure another double. In front of more than 67,000 spectators at the Stadio Olimpico in Rome, the Turin team needed almost the full extra time period to wait until the 110th minute for Alvaro Morata to get the better of Riccardo Montolivo's AC Milan.

At just 23 years of age, Paul already had plenty of trophies under his belt: two Italian Super Cups, four Italian league titles and two Italian cups.

On Tuesday 21 February 2016, Monaco travelled to the Etihad Stadium to play Manchester City in the Champions League last sixteen. 'To tell the truth,' explains James Robson, a reporter at the *Manchester Evening News*, 'we didn't know anything about Mbappé. During the press conference, Kevin De Bruyne even admitted he'd never heard of him.'

After the great performances of late December, Kylian kept up the pace at the start of the year. He scored one goal and provided two assists during two starts in the Coupe de France against AC Ajaccio and FC Chambly. He put his foot on the gas in February, scoring again against Montpellier, then coming away from Monaco's 5–0 win over FC Metz with a hat-trick. As a result, Leonardo Jardim gave him his first Champions League start in Manchester, supporting Radamel Falcao as centre forward.

'The English journalists didn't necessarily expect

to see him start, but the press box was very quickly won over.' With a perfect call and a lightning finish, Kylian scored his first Champions League goal in the 41st minute to give his team a 2–1 lead just before the break and become the second youngest French player to ever score in the Champions League (behind Karim Benzema). 'In the end, Manchester City won 5–3, but that took nothing away from Mbappé's performance. We understood why Pep Guardiola had put €40 million on the table to try to get a player who was completely unknown in England.'

His impressions were confirmed during the return leg of the last sixteen game two weeks later at the Stade Louis II. Kylian took charge of giving his team the best possible start by opening the scoring in the eighth minute on the end of a powerful cross in front of goal from Bernardo Silva. In the 29th minute, he initiated the frenetic counter-attack concluded by a winning shot from the inside of Fabinho's foot. Monaco qualified for the quarter-finals beating Manchester City 3–1.

Kylian continued his irresistible rise and against the Borussia Dortmund on 12 April 2017, he scored twice in a 3–2 win. To celebrate his two goals, for the first time Kylian performed the celebration that would be beamed around the world. Full of confidence, with his arms crossed and his chest and head held high. 'It came out of nothing, I was playing PlayStation with my little brother. He scored a goal and celebrated by doing this. Five minutes later, he stopped and said to me: "Kylian, you could do that in a match." So it happened in Dortmund and I did it.' Kylian would tell the beIN Sports microphones.

He would add another goal a week later, in the quarter-final return leg that Monaco eventually won 3–1. But his first European adventure would come to an end in Turin against Juventus in early May. 'In the first leg, I thought Mbappé was a little inhibited by the stakes,' said the *Tuttosport* journalist, Guido Vaciago. After a 2–0 defeat in the front of their own fans, Monaco had nothing left to lose: 'Juve did win again, but ... what I remember most is that he was the striker who had posed the biggest problems to our defence throughout the competition. Barzagli, who is famous in Serie A and in Europe for his pace, suffered like never before.'

His well-used right foot tricked Gigi Buffon in the 69th minute to score what would be his sixth and last goal in the 2016–17 Champions League campaign. As the final whistle blew, Kylian was obviously disappointed, but the wonderful embrace with the veteran Italian goalkeeper at the end of the game spoke volumes: in just a few months, he had forged both a name and a reputation on the international stage.

Chapter 8

Goodbye and hello

'I've spent ten incredible years here. I arrived a child and am leaving a man. You were the first and only ones to believe in me. It wasn't easy for me at Real to start with. After several years at the training academy, where I worked hard and sacrificed a lot, I made it to the first team with the sole aim of playing at the highest level. Once again, thanks to your unconditional support, I succeeded.

'I needed to set myself new goals and new challenges. This summer, Atlético offered me this opportunity … Believe me, even if I am no longer wearing a Real Sociedad shirt and not living in San Sebastián, I will never forget the time I have spent here.'

The farewell letter turned an important page in his life in order to open another, that of his adulthood and hopes for the future. It was 7pm on 28 July 2014 at the Zubieta when Antoine began speaking, reciting it from memory, during an impromptu press conference. After ten years at Real Sociedad, five seasons with the professionals, 202 matches played and 53 goals scored, the French player was flying the nest as the Madrid team managed to come to an agreement for the payment of his release clause of €30 million. He became the second most expensive player in the history of the Colchoneros. Only the Colombian Radamel Falcao, who had come from Porto for €42 million in 2011, had cost more.

From San Francisco, where they had just played the first match of their pre-season tour, Diego Simeone said: 'Griezmann will bring to the team the pace it has been lacking since the departure of Adrián, Costa and David Villa.' It was clear that, as far as the coaching staff were concerned, the French player would be the perfect second striker alongside Mario Mandžukić, newly arrived from Bayern Munich.

On 31 July 2014, under a blazing sun and stifling heat, Antoine climbed the steps to the pitch at the Vicente Calderón Stadium. He was wearing the red-and-white striped shirt, with the number 7 on the back. Six thousand supporters were sitting in the first ring of the stands with banners, Tricolore flags and smoke grenades to give the young man a fitting welcome to his new home. Griezmann started with some keepie uppies, like a magician with the ball at his feet, to the delight of the assembled photographers. And, while they immortalised the moment, Antoine took a selfie in front of the stand and posted it on Twitter.

The Frenchman made his debut for the Colchoneros on 10 August at the Volkswagen Arena, against

VfL Wolfsburg, in a friendly match. On 22 August, Antoine celebrated Atlético's victory in the Spanish Super Cup against Real Madrid at the Vicente Calderón Stadium. In the first leg, at the Santiago Bernabéu Stadium, the two teams were neck and neck, with the game finishing 1–1. During the return leg, only two minutes after kick-off, a Moya clearance made it half-way up the Merengues' midfield. Grizi headed it on to release Mandžukić, who found himself face-to-face with Iker Casillas. The giant Croatian did not waste the chance. The match finished with a 1–0 victory for Atlético.

On Tuesday 16 September in Piraeus against Olympiakos in the first Champions League game of the season, Grizi scored his first goal in a red-and-white striped shirt, only to reduce the score line during the first defeat of the season for Simeone's men (2–3). Atlético's number 7 would wait another month before scoring his second on 22 October, again in the Champions League, (5–0 against Malmö). On 1 November 2014, at home against FC Cordoba, the tenth match of the La Liga season, the Frenchman scored two goals in the same game for the first time with the Colchoneros. Now things were really heating up.

Griezmann's place in the starting eleven would still be up for discussion, and whenever he did start a game, he would always end up being substituted by Raúl García, Raúl Jimenez or Saul in the second half. 'The manager always asks us to up the intensity, both at training and on match days. As far as we were concerned, we saw right at the start that Antoine would become an extremely important player in the team,' said Tiago, 'but Simeone is a demanding manager.'

Griezmann won the trust of his manager on Sunday 21 December 2014 at the San Mamés. Against Athletic Bilbao, the number 7, who had abandoned his boy-next-door look in favour of a platinum blond crest on a black background, scored a hat-trick to wipe the floor with the Basques. From that moment on, the Frenchman was launched at high speed through a season that was completely exceptional. In January, February and March, he scored eight goals, just as he did in five of six matches in April, including two goals on three occasions. These performances earned him the title of player of the month in La Liga, a title he had already won in January. The curtain fell on the 84th Spanish championship on 23 May. Atlético finished in third place, sixteen points behind the champions, Barcelona.

In the Copa del Rey, the Blaugrana knocked out the Colchoneros in the quarter-finals, while Real Madrid took care of eliminating them from the Champions League at the same stage. Griezmann did however clinch the Onze d'Or prize for the best French player of the year, beating Paul Pogba and Alexandre Lacazette. And with 25 goals between La Liga, the Copa del Rey and the Champions League, he fell just behind Diego

Forlán (32), Radamel Falcao (28) and Diego Costa (27) as the top scorer for Atlético in a single season.

His second year in the Spanish capital had an absolutely fantastic start: 22 goals in 38 Liga matches, three goals in the Copa del Rey and seven goals in thirteen Champions League matches. In addition, on 8 April 2016, Antoine received the greatest of gifts: Erika gave birth to Mia, his daughter. 'She's so beautiful, I can't find the words,' he told the press.

Five days later, the second leg of the Champions League quarter-final match between the Colchoneros and the Blaugrana was played at the Vicente Calderón. Simeone's team had to overturn a 2–1 deficit at home to avoid being eliminated. The French player scored twice yet again. His first came with a header from a Saul cross in the 36th minute thanks to a particularly impressive move: Antoine jumped up into the air to deflect the ball, climbing so high he was unreachable, while Gérard Pique and Dani Alves could only watch. His second came from the penalty spot in the 88th minute of a match that was 'the best of my career from an emotional point of view,' according to Antoine.

On 3 May, Bayern Munich played host to Atlético Madrid at the Allianz Arena for the return leg of the semi-final. Xabi Alonso gave Pep Guardiola's Germans the advantage with a free-kick, putting the two teams level on aggregate. But Griezmann had other ideas. By the centre circle, he picked out Fernando Torres, who immediately headed the ball on. Flirting with the offside rule, the French player penetrated his opponents half unmarked. 'In my head I was telling myself that what I had to do was open up my foot. So, I positioned myself slightly to the side, moved and eventually scored,' Antoine said after the match. The Bavarians won the game 2–1 but it was Atlético who qualified for the final.

The Champions League final was held on 28 May 2016 at the San Siro in Milan. In the fifteenth minute the Merengues took the lead thanks to a goal from Sergio Ramos. By half time, the score remained unchanged, even if Griezmann had tried everything: right foot, left foot, up close and from distance. At the very start of the second half, Pepe fouled Torres in the box. The referee, Mark Clattenburg, blew the whistle and pointed to the spot. It fell to Antoine Griezmann to take the kick.

The Red and Whites' number 7 gathered himself, darted forward and shot with his left foot. 'Boom!' The shot was clean and hard and left no room for questions. The ball crashed against the crossbar, before bouncing off into the distance towards the middle of the Colchoneros half. Navas threw himself to the left. He was completely beaten, but the ball, which had only to slip under the crossbar, smashed against it by just a few centimetres.

'For at least a week, I couldn't get that penalty out of my mind. I took and retook it so many times,'

Griezmann would admit during an interview with *Onda Cero*. 'I'm convinced we would have won the Champions League if I'd scored it.' Although he had not managed to equalise, the Belgian, Yannick Carrasco would take care of it in the 78th minute. The score was still 1–1 at full time and remained the same after extra time. It was time for penalties.

Real began. Lucas Vázquez converted. One–nil.

It was already Antoine's turn. He took the ball, placed it on the eleven-metre spot and did not break his gaze. The keeper went one way, the ball the other. One–one. Gone were the demons. But this time the outcome did not depend on him alone. A grimace, a raised thumb and the duel between these two rival clubs continued.

Marcelo, Gabi, Bale, Saul and Ramos made no mistake. Four–three, but Juanfran struck the post.

Next up was Cristiano Ronaldo, the Merengues number 7. His strike would wrong-foot Oblak. 'Antoine started crying and we all crumbled,' said Théo, who was sitting in the stands at the San Siro alongside other members of Antoine's family. The emotions were overwhelming when Simeone came over and hugged Antoine in the middle of the pitch.

On 13 June 2017, Antoine Griezmann agreed to renew the contract binding him to Atlético Madrid, extending his relationship with the Colchoneros by one more year, until June 2022. The announcement from Atlético put an end to a soap opera that had kept the team's fans holding their breath.

It was reported in January that Manchester United were prepared to pay the €100 million release clause in Antoine's contract and offer him a salary somewhere in the region of €17 million a year. It was also rumoured that Paul Pogba had personally committed to convincing his friend to embark on a new adventure in England. According to *L'Équipe* on 8 April 2017, the day before the derby, Real Madrid were also courting Griezmann. At the end of the match at the Bernabéu in which he scored the goal to secure a draw, Antoine answered: 'No, I'm not ruling anything out but I'm happy at Atlético.'

So why was there so much insistence and so many transfer rumours about the French player? Unfortunately, titles during the 2016–17 season had vanished into thin air one after the other. Atlético had finished third in La Liga. They had been knocked out of the Copa del Rey in the semi-final by Barcelona and suffered yet another humiliation at the hands of Real in the semi-final of the Champions League. Antoine had scored 26 goals in 53 games, a total of 83 in three seasons for Atlético, but his accolades at club level were few and far between.

But it was not to be for the 2017–18 season. Things became clear on 4 June when the Court of Arbitration for Sport confirmed the sanction imposed on Atlético by FIFA. Due to irregularities in the recruitment of

65 players at U14 level, the Madrid club would not be able to purchase any new footballers until the end of January 2018. It was what Griezmann had been waiting for in order to make his decision. 'It's a difficult time for the club. It would be a dirty move to leave now. We've spoken with the directors and we will be back next season.'

Nine days later, the contract that would take his salary, if the rumours are to be believed, to €10 million a year, was signed. Griezmann would yet again be the key player for the club, which, after 50 years, would be moving from the Vicente Calderón to the new Wanda Metropolitano stadium.

However, Antoine's decision to stay at Atlético did have consequences. Éric Olhats split with his protégé after twelve years. 'The recent decisions about Griezmann's image and future are not compatible with how I envisaged our professional relationship. From now on I will focus on my role as a scout for Real Sociedad,' he told *L'Equipe*.

In a ceremony that took the media by surprise, Antoine Griezmann married Erika Choperena on Thursday 15 June 2017 in Toledo. The wedding would be extremely private. Photographers and TV cameras were not allowed into the 11th-century Palacio de Galiana on the banks of the Tagus and the only guests were family and close friends, as well as a handful of teammates.

*

On 16 September, Grizi went down in Atletico history by victoriously turning in a cross from Ángel Correa at the near post. It was the first ever goal at the brand new Wanda Metropolitano and marked a win against Málaga. Unfortunately, the first part of the season would pass Antoine by and he failed to score another goal in La Liga until mid-November. Things were no better in the Champions League, where Atlético were unceremoniously dumped into the Europa League.

But the Frenchman lit up that competition from the early rounds, with three goals and three assists. One small footnote: on 5 April 2018 against Sporting Lisbon, he did not greet his goal with his traditional tribute to the Canadian rapper, Drake. This time, he started dancing in a fashion that could well have confused those unfamiliar with video games: with the thumb and forefinger of his right hand, he held up an L to his forehead while jumping from one foot to the other. This choreography was inspired by the hit adventure game *Fortnite* and it was to become the signature move of this new Grizou, who had abandoned his long blonde tresses for an ultra-short haircut.

The semi-final duel against Arsenal was wonderful to see during the first leg on 26 April at the Emirates Stadium. In the 61st minute, Lacazette jumped at the far post to head a cross from Wilshere. The bounce got the better of Oblak. One–nil, with Atlético down to ten men. But in the 81st minute, Grizou stood up to be counted: on the end of a long, deep ball he forced

Koscielny into an error. Ospina turned his first strike away but the ball rebounded to Antoine's feet and all he had to do was fire it into the back of the net. It was a miracle goal that allowed Atlético to content themselves with a narrow 1–0 win in the return leg to reach their third European final in five years.

The final against Marseille was played on 21 May 2018 at the Grand Stade de Lyon. In the 21st minute, following an ill-judged clearance from Mandanda, Grizou punished the keeper with an unstoppable left-footed shot. One–nil. In the 49th minute, thanks to an assist from Koke, Antoine once again made it into the penalty area to score his second with a magnificent flick of his left foot. Two–nil. Gabi added the third in the 89th minute and Antoine finally savoured his first European title on the pitch. The Frenchman was unquestionably the Man of the Match, with two goals that brought his total to 29 for the season in a Colchoneros shirt.

At 1.21am Italian time on 9 August 2016, Manchester United pulled off a Hollywood-style move, launching a nine-second online video with the message 'Are you ready? Pogback.' In the darkness, Paul is wearing a United sweatshirt with his hood up, *Assassin's Creed* style. The traditional statement was issued at 1.35am: 'Manchester United are delighted to announce that Paul Pogba has completed his transfer from Italian club Juventus. Paul joins on a five-year contract, with the option to extend for a further year.'

It was the Turin club who made the transfer figures official: 'Juventus Football Club S.p.A announces the agreement with Manchester United Football Club Limited for the definitive transfer of the sporting services of the footballer Paul Labile Pogba for a sum of €105 million,' an unprecedented figure in the history of football. Paul Pogba would earn €14 million per season for five years, plus image rights.

The ex-number 10 would send a video message in Italian to his former fans: 'It's a bit of a sad moment because I'm going to another team … I would like to thank Juventus: the footballers, fans and staff for believing in me. You will always be in my heart, thank you again.' Juventus responded by publishing a video of his play and finest goals, accompanied by the hashtag #MerciPaul.

To his new fans Paul wrote: 'I am delighted to re-join United. It has always been a club with a special place in my heart and I am really looking forward to working with José Mourinho.'

Paul was welcomed. The Red Devils fans saw him as one of their own, the prodigal son returned home. He had won so many people over, particularly the kids lining the streets around the stadium proudly wearing his number 6 red shirt. Despite that, the assessments of the French player's first season at United were not conclusively positive. In the *Red News* fanzine, Sparky's 'End of Season Squad Review' claimed: 'Let's be honest, he's been a bit of disappointment, hasn't he? Not to say he won't get better, but people expecting a game-dominating monster were surely disappointed.' And they were not the only ones. Frank Lampard, the former Chelsea midfielder, told Sky Sports Monday Night Football: 'Pogba's got fantastic attributes. He's strong, he's got great feet, he's bigger than you and he's quicker than you as a midfield player. But when you have a £90 million price tag on your shoulders, we analyse more and we want more.'

His father, Fassou Antoine Pogba, had died following a long illness on 12 May at the age of 79. On Tuesday 17 May, Paul, Mathias and Florentin, alongside Antoine Fassou's other children, family members and friends, had attended his funeral in Roissy-en-Brie. The day after the ceremony, Paul paid tribute to his father on Instagram with a video: filmed at home on the sofa, Paul tried to teach his father to Dab. It was accompanied by a brief caption – 'RIP Papa' – and a heart emoji.

Yet, on the eve of the final league game and the Europa League final, the United faithful continued to believe in him. No one was shouting 'So much money wasted'; at most they ventured a 'Come on, show us you're worth what we paid for you.' Paul Labile Pogba did not disappoint them and, after his worst season since 2012–13 (eight goals, 50 matches), he at least played his part in the Europa League win.

During his second season at the Red Devils since his famous return, the 'Pogback' effect had fizzled out.

Despite an encouraging start, the midfielder had fallen victim to a hamstring injury in September that kept him out for several weeks. On 31 January against Tottenham, the worst happened with almost 30 minutes gone, when Paul came over to the touchline to talk to Mourinho. The verbal exchange had no visible results on the pitch, Paul was substituted in the 63rd minute and the *Sun* reported a dressing room bust-up between a furious Mourinho and Phil Jones and Paul Pogba after one of the following games at Newcastle.

The United squad failed to get past Sevilla in the Champions League last sixteen and they were never in contention for the Premier League. Second in the table behind their local rivals Manchester City, the Red Devils saw their consolation prize of the FA Cup vanish from under their noses on 19 May at Wembley, when Mourinho's side were defeated by Conte's Chelsea (1–0). Paul would be named player of the month in April – five games, three goals, two assists and two Man of the Match awards – but there was little more to celebrate.

Only four days had passed since the French title had been decided and Kylian was already having to answer the question of the summer: Where would he play next season? Alongside him on the makeshift TV set was Vadim Vasilyev, who promised: 'We're going to do everything we can to keep him.'

It was nothing new: Kylian had been attracting the interest of big European clubs since he was fourteen.

Florentino Pérez – the president of Real Madrid – was one of those who had fallen for his charms; in early May, the *Guardian* reported that Manchester United had offered £72 million for Mbappé and that Manchester City were getting ready to put £143 million on the table. He also topped the wish lists of Juventus, Manchester City, Arsenal, Liverpool and PSG.

On 26 July, *Marca* took aim on its front page: 'Agreement in principle for Mbappé: 180 million. The Frenchman could become the most expensive signing in the history of football … the young French player will sign [with Real Madrid] for six seasons, during each of which he will earn €7 million.' On 3 August, PSG officially announced the signing of Neymar Junior: €222 million and around €36 million a year for the player. Everything seemed clear to the media. PSG were now out of the running; Manchester City and Arsenal had given up … it was only a matter of days before Kylian would sign for Real Madrid.

But, according to the Madrid press, Monaco wanted more money. In addition, Zidane could only see a deal with Mbappé working if Bale left. On 10 August, two sources on either side of the Pyrenees were in agreement: 'Unless the situation changes, we can confirm that @KMbappe is coming to Paris,' announced *ParisUnited*, a website from the French capital that always has its ear to the ground. *Marca* confirmed: 'The impossible is about to happen. Kylian Mbappé will become a PSG player. Case closed.'

Wilfrid Mbappé and Antero Henrique, PSG's sporting director, had apparently come to an agreement
in principle based on a five-year contract and a gross
annual salary of €18 million, the club's second highest.
Mbappé senior had also been reassured about Financial
Fair Play, as Antero Henrique calmed him down by
guaranteeing that PSG had the financial means to cope
with another multimillion-euro deal.

No one in Monaco was happy about it. In order
to protect his number 29 from the media whirlwind,
Jardim overlooked Kylian for the league games against
Metz and OM. Some media outlets were also reporting
that there had been a training ground bust-up between
Kylian and Andrea Raggi, something that was said to
have resulted in the striker being sent off.

Monaco entered negotiations with PSG and, despite
initially accepting the proposal from the Parisian club,
they later retracted it and vetoed the transfer. So
much so that overnight between 30 and 31 August,
there was still no talk of an agreement. But at 6.30pm
on 31 August 2017, a photo of Kylian appeared on
the principality club's website with a two-line caption: 'AS Monaco wish all the best for the future to
@KMbappe who is joining @PSG_inside! #MerciKylian'.

A minute later it was the turn of the club in the
capital: 'Paris Saint-Germain are delighted to announce
the signing of Kylian Mbappé! #BienvenueKylian.'
After four years, almost two seasons as a professional,
58 games, 27 goals and sixteen assists, the little gem of

French football was saying goodbye to the principality. He arrived in Paris on the basis of a season-long loan, with a subsequent purchase option of €180 million. This formula allowed PSG to circumvent the risk of contravening Financial Fair Play regulations. Mbappé would sign a contract tying him to the Parisian club until 30 June 2022 and become the second most expensive footballer in footballing history, behind Neymar, and the most expensive transfer between two French clubs.

On 6 September, there was a full house in the auditorium at the Parc des Princes for the official unveiling of PSG's new player. Wearing a dark blue suit, white shirt and dark tie, an elegant and formal outfit, the eighteen year old began his monologue: 'Hello everyone. As you know, it's a great pleasure for me to be joining PSG, one of the best clubs in the world ... It's also important to come home, to the city where I was born and where I grew up. With PSG, with lots of hard work, respect and humility, we can achieve our goals of winning lots of trophies and the dream that drives everyone at the club: the Champions League.'

This was followed by thanks to his family, lawyers and everyone at PSG who had helped make his transfer a reality. Next came the turn of the journalists' questions from all sides about Unai Emery, his new manager; about Neymar and how much his arrival at PSG had influenced Kylian's decision; about how prepared he was to handle the pressure. There was something for everyone and, of course, there was the small matter of the €180 million.

'That question comes up a lot and I always have the same response,' said Kylian. 'I don't handle everything, it's not my job, so it's not something I deal with. The price is by-the-by as far as I'm concerned. It's not going to change how I live or think, and even less how I play.'

After some photos, he stepped out onto the red carpet outside the stadium to greet the fans. Wearing an '*Ici, c'est Paris*' scarf, he shook hands, signed autographs, took photos, bowed and even jumped up and down. '*Mbappé allez, allez, allez*!' sang the ultras. Kylian the Communicator played along.

But he got off to a bad start, and criticism started after the away game at Dijon on 14 October. 'For the first time since exploding in Ligue 1, Kylian disappointed us.' 'Invisible for the first 45 minutes, he made a startling number of mistakes in the second half.' 'He made some uncharacteristic mistakes in front of goal.' The media and pundits did not hold back.

The worst was yet to come. And come it did in the evening of Sunday 22 October against OM at the Vélodrome. 'Mbappé played his worst match since joining PSG'; 'Without a doubt, his worst performance for a year'. It was not only his performance on the pitch that attracted the wrath of the press, there was also the fact that the new PSG player had shown a different side to himself during a row. After the final whistle, Kylian, cautioned for having taken the referee by the arm to demand a penalty, accused the man in black of being 'substandard'.

But by all appearances, Kylian did not seem unduly concerned. He turned nineteen on 20 December 2017. He decided to change his hair colour for the occasion and had it dyed blond. His birthday was celebrated that same evening at the Parc des Princes. It was the nineteenth game of the season, a perfect coincidence and an excuse to put on a show. In the 21st minute, he got past two defenders and put his foot down with lightning speed on the right wing to overtake Da Silva before looking up, seeing Cavani in the area and sending him a cross. The Uruguayan finished with a back-heel worthy of Madjer. Stunning! One–nil PSG. In the 57th minute, Neymar picked up the ball on the left for a pass to Lo Celso, who had sneaked into the area and just about managed to keep the ball from going out for a goal kick before making his cross. With a left-footed volley, Mbappé showed no mercy to Rémy Vercoutre, the Caen keeper. The game, the last of the year, finished 3–1 to the Parisians. Kylian was man of the match. It brought an end to an impressive December: four goals and three assists in five games.

He was celebrating a crazy 2017: 33 goals for club and country across all competitions (twenty with Monaco, twelve with PSG and one with Les Bleus) to top the list of French scorers of the year, ahead of

Alexandre Lacazette, with 32, and Antoine Griezmann with 29. He had scored ten goals in the Champions League and was the youngest footballer to have ever achieved such a feat.

However, in the run-up to the first leg of the last sixteen game against Real Madrid, Kylian was in far from his best form, having scored only one goal against Dijon in the league on 17 January. His game got off to a timid start to say the least, but in the 33rd minute, he was responsible for breaking the deadlock: his pass from the right wing was dealt with poorly by Nacho and Adrien Rabiot surged forward to punish Keylor Navas. Nil–one. It was enough to needle Cristiano Ronaldo. The five-time Ballon d'Or-winner brought the score line back to 1–1 in the dying moments of the first half by converting a penalty with a powerful strike. But when play resumed, it was the Frenchman's turn to shine: Neymar's service was impeccable but Kylian's shot lacked accuracy and Navas parried it as best he could. Missed! At the end of the game, Ronaldo scored a second with his knee before Marcelo made things 3–1. The disappointment was huge for the PSG number 29, especially as, right at the end of the game, he could have made it 3–2 and thrown the last sixteen tie back in the balance, but Real's Costa Rican goalkeeper came out on top for a second time.

The young Parisian striker only had one thing on his mind: getting his revenge two weeks later at the Parc des Princes. Unfortunately, preparation for the second

(top left) At the start of his second season with Real Sociedad, Griezmann had become the darling of the supporters, but he was not fit enough to make the starting eleven until 18 September 2011, where he scored against Real Madrid at the Anoeta Stadium.
Juan Herrero/Epa/Shutterstock

(top right) On 20 September 2011, Pogba made his professional debut with Manchester United against Leeds United in the Carling Cup at Elland Road.
Phil Oldham/Shutterstock

Kylian Mbappé scored his first goal for Monaco's first team on 20 February 2016. In his ninth appearance for the team, he became the youngest professional goalscorer in the history of AS Monaco.
Lionel Cironneau/AP/Shutterstock

(*above*) Both Pogba and Griezmann played in their first ever World Cup game for France, against Honduras, on 15 June 2014 in Brazil. Antoinne narrowly missed scoring, but Paul won a penalty, which led to Benzema opening the scoring. France won the match 3–0.
Laurentvu/Taamallah/Sipa/Shutterstock

Celebrating a goal against Marseille in the UEFA Europa League Final on 16 May 2018, Antoinne shows off his new *Fortnite*-inspired signature move – holding up an L to his forehead while jumping from one foot to the other.
BPI/Shutterstock

Chapter 9

Pick a game

'When Antoine was fourteen, he was a Lyon fan,' Alain Griezmann told Spanish journalist Javier Villagarcía. 'If someone had said to me back then that my son would play for Real Sociedad, I would have told them they were mad! But now they're Antoine's team. It's the same for me ... They're the ones who had faith in him and gave him his chance.'

Imagine the excitement when, on Friday 9 August 2013, at the stroke of noon, the draw for the preliminary round of the Champions League was made and Lyon–Real Sociedad came out of the hat. 'The opponents I wanted,' Antoine said at the press conference that followed. It was the opportunity to chase away his old demons once and for all against what had once been his favourite club and to finally step out onto the pitch at the Stade de Gerland, something he had dreamed about so often as a kid. There was also an incredible quirk of fate: on 10 March 2004, he had been in the stands at the Stade de Gerland for Real Sociedad's last European game. The Basque team were beaten 1–0 and sent packing by Olympique Lyonnais in the return leg of the Champions League knock-out round. That night, Antoine had told his father that he 'wanted to play in those kind of matches one day'.

Nine years later his dream had come true. On 20 August 2013, Olympique Lyonnais and Real Sociedad took to the pitch in front of 40,000 specta- tors. Antoine was the last to climb the stairs to face the public. His hair was dyed completely blond, as it was when he had had his trial aged thirteen. The images of his failures and the battles he had since won must have been running through his mind when the official anthem of the Champions League began to ring out. Antoine glanced at the Jean-Jaures stand, where his friends and family were. He was trying to find his father, who must have been filled with emotion to finally see his son play on the turf at the Stade de Gerland.

The music came to an end. The Griezmann show could begin. In the fifth minute, Liassine Cadamuro picked out Antoine with a long pass down the left wing. It was almost his first touch. He controlled it just beyond the midfield, then embarked on a lengthy run along the touchline to flummox his man-marker, Miguel Lopes. Antoine got around him, lifted his head and found Carlos Vela in space. The Mexican's strike just missed the goal. The French team had been given a warning. In the sixteenth minute, Vela, who had hit the post four minutes earlier, was at the heart of a move that saw the commentator get carried away: 'Vela is in an offside position but hasn't been spotted. He tries to find Griezmann who goes in with a bicycle kick – and opens the scoring with a magnificent strike by Real Sociedad's French player. What a goal! As a child he dreamt of playing in the Champions League for OL and now he's scored the first goal of tonight's game with an unforgettable move. The boy from Mâcon has helped Real Sociedad strike an important blow.'

On the bench, Arrasate had no need for the onslaught of slow motion replays to savour the talent of his striker: 'He jumped with such beauty, harmony and athleticism to strike the ball with his left foot and find the back of the net … It was one of the best goals he had ever scored. It was also very important.' Antoine did not stop there. In the 23rd minute, he found himself on the end of a long clearance from his keeper Claudio Bravo and in a tussle with Gueida Fofana. He managed to hold off his former France youth team teammate before unleashing a tight-angled left-footed shot that Anthony Lopes somehow managed to keep out.

'He knew how to use that pressure and turn it into something positive,' continues Arrasate. 'His goal, as well as his overall performance, helped him be seen in a new light in France, because his potential was already well known in Spain.' In the second half, the Basques scored a second goal in the 50th minute with a stunning strike from Seferović. Antoine played his part with the penultimate pass. In the 70th minute, he was replaced by Chori Castro. His return to France had not disappointed.

Paul would play his best match of the 2017–18 season on 7 April at the Etihad Stadium, during the 3–2 win over Manchester City that would delay the Sky Blues' coronation as Premier League champions.

No one would have bet on United at half-time, with the scoreboard showing 2–0 in favour of Pep Guardiola's men. After the break, the rafters were shook by a thunderous cheer: 97 seconds was all it took Paul Pogba to equalise. A close-range strike after Ander Herrera laid it off with his chest, followed by a powerful header over the top of Nicolás Otamendi that ricocheted off the right post of Ederson's goal. Pogba celebrated by cupping his hand behind his ear, as if to say 'I can't hear you'. It was a gesture of protest, an image he had already shared on social media the previous week following Guardiola's assertions in a press conference that Mino Raiola had offered to sell him the midfielder from Roissy-en-Brie during the January transfer window. He repeated his gesture on the pitch. He had a message to send.

The image says it all: Kylian, wearing a short-sleeved red and white shirt with both arms raised and his index fingers pointing up to the sky. His head is impeccably shaved and his black eyes are fixed on the stands. His face is calm. The former Bondy player no longer has to apologise for existing. He has probably already realised that this Friday 21 October 2016 will change the course of his young career. In the space of 90 minutes he has just demonstrated the incredible extent of his talents.

'Leonardo Jardim thought it was the right time to give him a second chance,' said an AS Monaco insider. 'He was happy with his attitude in the reserve team game the previous weekend … the calendar was starting to look busy and Jardim needed to find alternatives upfront.' Here was the number 29, not yet eighteen, walking out onto the pitch of the Stade Louis II to take his position upfront alongside his Colombian captain, Radamel Falcao. In the eleventh minute, Kylian sounded the revolt after Montpellier opened the scoring. Taking great strides, he went on a run down the left wing. This solo raid ended with a cross to the near post aimed at the head of Bernardo Silva, but it missed by a few inches. Kylian went unrewarded but it was the kind of move that inspired confidence and pointed to what was yet to come.

In the 35th minute, he would make the difference again and this time his marker was pushed to foul him on the left-hand edge of the area. Penalty! Radamel Falcao wrong-footed the Montpellier keeper to equalise, making it 1–1. The party was just getting started: only four minutes after the start of the second half, Mbappé surged towards the far post, quicker yet again than his opposite number, to fire an unstoppable header just past the right post. During the last half hour of the game, Kylian was the architect of two more goals. In the 74th minute, he supplied Valère Germain with a flawless cross to make it 4–2, then, two minutes later, provided another ball from the left wing, this time for Thomas Lemar to take advantage. Six–two and what a stunning game for Mbappé!

After the match, Kylian gave the media a clear and lucid analysis of the delicate situation he had been in since the start of his first professional season: 'I'm happy. When I don't play, it's always frustrating because I'm a competitor. But I'm here to learn and I spend a lot of time listening to advice from the other players.'

Chapter 10

Playing style

Antoine Griezmann

Martín Lasarte, his first coach for the Real Sociedad senior team:

> 'What surprised me about Antoine was his relaxation, the ease with which he adapted to a new situation … He worked along the wings, combining with midfielders, accelerating, dribbling, crossing well, standing out and finishing with accuracy and power. He had a great left foot and also fared well with his right.'

Carlos Bueno, teammate and friend:

> 'Every day after training, we would stay on the pitch for an extra hour. We would work on crosses, over and over, headers, free kicks and finishing … I like to tell myself that I taught him how to improve his relaxation, to hang in the air, to anticipate the

movement of his opponent. I used to say to Antoine: size doesn't matter.'

Roberto López Ufarte, legendary Real Sociedad player nicknamed 'The Little Devil':

'Whenever a small left-footed player came up from the Real academy, they would compare him to me and give him the same nickname. But I have to admit that Antoine, like every player who plays at the professional level nowadays, is better than those who played in my day. He strikes the ball better than I did, with more power, and is a better goal scorer than I was. But it's not only that: he knows how to organise the game, how to create space for his teammates and create opportunities. He's also very competitive. When he doesn't score, he just keeps on working until luck smiles on him again.'

Jagoba Arrasate, his last coach in San Sebastián:

'He was extremely versatile and had the gift of being in the right place at the right time. He would appear out of nowhere, when no one was expecting him. That always surprised defenders. He was a kid with plenty of maturity and he deserved everything he earned.'

Diego Simeone, his coach at Atlético de Madrid:

'He is the best footballer in the world when it comes to movement and knowing how to find space.'

'As far as I'm concerned,' he added when talking about 2016, 'Griezmann has been the best player in Europe.'

Paul Pogba

Paul McGuinness, his first coach at the Manchester United Academy:

'I soon saw he had quick footwork, great ball skills, timing, the ability to drop his shoulder and a lot of confidence. Above all he showed great personality.'

La Gazzetta dello Sport, on his arrival in Turin:

'The new Vieira and the fake Balotelli.'

Paul himself, to Sky Sports:

'I'm a technical player, despite how tall I am. I'm good at shooting but I like being on the ball. I take my inspiration from Vieira and everyone tells me I'm a lot like him. Physically, I've been mistaken for Balotelli. But I think I look more like Mario's brother.'

Patrick Vieira, to *France Football* in March 2014:

'Compared to me, Pogba is more attacking, whereas I was more defensively-minded. He pushes forward more and therefore scores more goals. He is also better on a technical level and is certainly more talented than I was … In a three-man midfield I think it suits his style of football'

José Mourinho, when Paul arrived at Man U:

'Paul will be a key part of the United team I want to build here for the future. He is quick, strong, scores goals and reads the game better than many players much older than he is. At 23, he has the chance to make that position his own here over many years. He is young and will continue to improve; he has the chance to be at the heart of this club for the next decade and beyond.'

Manchester United legend Wayne Rooney:

'For me Paul Pogba is a classic box-to-box player. He can do a bit of everything really well. If he has that freedom where he doesn't have to think too much about his defensive role he can cause mayhem.'

Kylian Mbappé

Gérard Prêcheur, former director of the INF
Clairefontaine:

> 'On the ball, he combined technical skill with speed
> of execution, which is very rare at that age, and he
> also had this natural side to him that tried not to
> be conventional. He knew what he wanted: "To be
> a professional footballer", "to be one of the best",
> "to win the Ballon d'Or".'

> 'With Thierry Henry it was his physical qualities that
> prevailed, whereas for Kylian it was his talent as a
> dribbler that emerged first.'

Bruno Irlès, his first coach at AS Monaco Academy:

> 'He immediately showed great potential going
> forward, in his footwork and technical ease with
> the ball. I also quickly noticed deficiencies in his
> defensive work, an area where he didn't make any
> effort at all.'

Frédéric Barilaro, his coach at the Monaco U19:

> 'He's most comfortable on the left wing, where he
> can do whatever he likes: cross, shoot or dribble. He
> can use both feet and his game is more developed
> than when he started. Kylian has some baffling

qualities, particularly when it comes to his ball skills.'

'I fought with him in training to get him to use his head sometimes. It's his weakness and I would often tease him about it. It's the mark of a great player.'

Diego Torres, Spanish journalist (*El País*), after Real Madrid–PSG on February 2018:

'Every time he touched the ball, something happened. He confirmed what I'd said about him in an article entitled "The Gazelle and the Panther". In my opinion, he was the perfect modern striker because he was the only one who combined, from the outset, the technique of Zidane and Benzema with the agility and speed of Thierry Henry and Samuel Eto'o. The comparison may have been daring but it soon became clear we were dealing with an exceptional player.'

Chapter 10

Bleus and 'Bleuets'

There was barely time to savour his first year in Real Sociedad's first team when a new challenge presented itself for Antoine Griezmann: the U19 European Championships with the France team, played at home, in Normandy, in July 2010.

In early March that year, he had been called up for the first time for two friendlies against the Ukraine. Snubbed by the French training academies five years earlier, Antoine was preparing to join the elite of the 1991 generation, including the promising captain Gueida Fofana and the phenomenon Gaël Kakuta; not to mention the Lyonnais gang, with Sébastien Faure, Timothée Kolodziejczak, Enzo Reale, and Alexandre Lacazette.

Francis Smerecki – the manager then – 'had his favourites', remembers the central defender Sébastien Faure 'and the squad had barely changed in two years. We knew that Antoine had played regularly in the Spanish second division, but not much more than that. He was unknown to most of the players on the team, except Clément [Grenier] and Alex [Lacazette], who immediately recognised him.' The hours spent on the pitch during his trial at the Plaine des Jeux de Gerland in Lyon had not been in vain after all: at least they helped ease his integration into the France team.

By dinner time, 'The Spaniard' was already sur-rounded and at his ease when his teammates began to tap their knives against their glasses. It was time for his initiation: a classic in football for any new player joining a team. 'Sing, sing, sing!' the group chanted in unison. The striker got up from his chair and turned to face his teammates. Quick as a flash, he started singing 'La Bamba': an old favourite and a guaranteed crowd-pleaser! There was laughing, whistling and clapping. 'La Bamba' had helped Grizou score points. Now he just had to prove himself on the pitch.

Antoine was in Francis Smerecki's starting eleven for the first two group matches: 4–1 and 5–0 wins over the Netherlands and Austria respectively. France held their own in their group, finishing with a 0–0 draw against England. The team met Croatia in the semi-final in a game that went down to the wire. Antoine was all over the pitch, leaping on Cédric Bakambu when the Sochaux player scored the winning goal in the 83rd minute. Two–one and Les Bleus were in the final. The pleasure was two-fold as there they would play Spain, who had humiliated them two years earlier during the U17 Euros.

Thirtieth July 2010. The Stade Michel d'Ornano,

where Stade Malherbe de Caen play their home games, was packed to the rafters with 21,000 spectators, including the players' friends and family, representatives of French football and the President of UEFA, Michel Platini. Griezmann started on the left wing in a strike force that included Gilles Sunu on the right, Cédric Bakambu up front and Gaël Kakuta in support.

Antoine, of course, knew almost all the opposing players as he had played against them in the Spanish youth leagues, but during the first 45 minutes of the final, he seemed lost on the pitch. Unable to make the right choices, overwhelmed, jostled, helpless in the face of the short passing game instigated by the Roja. At half time, it came as no surprise that Spain were leading 1–0.

Griezmann's head was down as he returned to the dressing room. Fifteen minutes later he failed to reappear on the pitch. Was this his manager's choice? Apparently not. His ankle was troubling him too much and he was replaced. In the 49th minute, his replacement, Yannis Tafer, sent Gilles Sunu through perfectly into space to equalise, 1–1. The second, in the 85th minute when the stadium started shaking after a throw-in from Kakuta was headed towards the far post by Lacazette. 'Champions of Europe!' With his flip-flops and injured ankle, Antoine was the last to join the melée of players that had formed near a corner post. He was struggling to hold back his tears. A few months ago, he had been the forgotten man of French football.

Here he was, an U19 European champion and, along-side the others of the 1991 generation, a new standard-bearer for French football.

Unlike Griezmann, Paul Pogba had been a key player in the French youth teams since an early age. After his debut in the Val-de-Marne tournament when he was spotted by Manchester United, he was selected to play in the U17 European Championships held in Liechtenstein in May 2010.

After a loss against Spain on 18 May (2–1), Les Bleuets' number 6 did what was expected of him against Portugal and played his best match of the year in a France shirt; a deflected shot from him decided the match. France won 1–0 and, on beating Switzerland three days later (3–1), qualified for the semi-final. Their adventure came to an end against England at the Rheinpark in Vaduz on 27 May. They were two goals down at half time. In the 56th minute, Pogba seemed to put things back in doubt after scoring a header on the end of a cross from Abdoulaye Doucouré, but in the end the French fell at the hands of the English, the eventual winners of the tournament. 'We lost but we learned. It was an experience that helped me grow,' Paul would later claim.

Wearing the captain's armband, Paul led the charge for France in the U19 European Championships in July 2012. It was a great experience that came to an end in the semi-final, in the Lilleküla Stadium in Tallinn, against Spain (3–3 after extra time, 4–2 to the Spaniards on penalties). The Roja won the title and Les Bleuets went home empty handed. 'Paul was one of the leaders of the team,' remembers Pierre Mankowski, the manager. 'He was very dynamic on the pitch. Against Serbia, in the first match, he scored a penalty to make it 2–0. He had a great match against Spain … He took the first penalty and scored to give us the lead. But then luck wasn't on our side.'

On 14 March 2013, the day before his twentieth birthday, Didier Deschamps called upon Juventus' young hopeful for two qualifying matches for the 2014 Brazil World Cup that were to be played four days apart at the Stade de France against Georgia and Spain. 'I have other players in the midfield but they don't have the same profile, particularly in terms of attacking efficiency,' explained the French senior team manager when he announced the squad. 'He's a player for the future and the future is being built today.'

On Saturday 22 March at Saint-Denis, Paul played for the full 90 minutes in the 3–1 win over Georgia. However, the present that had seemed so wonderful at first glance, soon turned sour the following Tuesday against the Roja, then both world and European champions. On the pitch at Saint-Denis, the Spanish opened the scoring in the 58th minute with a goal from Pedro. Paul did not let his head drop and worked hard to reduce spaces and disrupt the Spaniards' short, sharp passing game as best he could. He was determined to make his mark, unfortunately too determined. In the 77th minute, in a fiercely contested aerial battle with Xabi Alonso, he received a warning for a knee in the back of the future Bayern Munich player. Just one minute later, the France team's number 19 was given a second yellow card, this time for showing his studs in a late tackle on Xavi.

No French international player had ever been sent off in their second only match. In the post-match press conference, the kid from Roissy-en-Brie tried to ease his disappointment by talking to journalists about his premature exit: 'When I was sent off I hardly touched Xavi. But … that's football. I'm mad at myself for causing trouble for my team.' A few minutes earlier, in the dressing room, he apologised to his teammates, promising to learn his lesson.

A couple of month after, he was picked to take part in the U20 World Cup to be played in Turkey from 21 June to 13 July 2013. He was even named as one of the squad's leaders, alongside the Real Madrid defender Raphaël Varane. 'He arrived with a big smile on his face, delighted to be back among his friends,' admits Pierre Mankowski. 'He was already our captain before he went to play with the first team, and although he now had a different status, he remained the same and was fully committed.'

France started the competition on 21 June against Ghana, recent runners-up in the Africa Cup of Nations, at the Ali Sam Yen Arena in Istanbul. The France captain this time left it up to Kondogbia, Sanogo and Bahebeck to find the back of the net in the 3–1 win. Yaya Sanogo scored his second goal three days later against the United States but it was not enough to prevent France conceding a 1–1 draw and finding themselves in danger for the third and final group match against the Spanish team.

'We weren't in a good place before that match,' confirms teammate Naby Sarr. 'Especially because Paul was suspended.' The French captain had managed to collect two cautions against Ghana and the United States that kept him out of the decisive game. 'But despite his disappointment at not being on the pitch,' continues Pierre Mankowski, 'he played his role as captain all the same. I remember that at half time, he spoke to the group and said they couldn't possibly leave it at that ... In the end, we lost 2–1 but his intervention resonated throughout the competition.' Despite this defeat, France benefited from Ghana's decisive 4–1 win over the United States and finished second in Group A.

On 2 July, the small Kamil Ocak stadium in Gaziantep was jumping for the blockbuster game between Turkey and France. 'In an incredible atmosphere, we played a great match and won 4–1. We didn't give them any chances to believe and that gave us incredible strength for the rest of the competition,' says Mankowski. The return of Paul Pogba to the midfield was no coincidence when it came to the new side shown by the young French players.

In the semi-final, the number 6 stood firm and imposed himself on the midfield during the rematch against Ghana (2–1). On 13 July 2013, Pierre Mankowski's France returned to the Ali Sami Yen Stadium in Istanbul to face Uruguay, who had beaten a surprising Iraq team in the semi-final. Paul was not overawed at all; on the contrary, he used the pressure to produce football of the highest level. 'He was everywhere against Uruguay,' remembers Naby Sarr, who lined up in the central defence alongside Kurt Zouma in the final. 'He showed that he was already a great player. He swept up the ball and gave it back to you cleanly every time. He was also very active offensively. He was the nerve centre of our team.' Pierre Mankowski confirms: 'He was everywhere and it wasn't surprising. That was his character. As long as I've known him, he has wanted to be the best midfielder, the best defender, the best striker and, if he could, the best goalkeeper. That's Paul Pogba.'

No goals were scored during the 90 minutes or during extra time. 'Obviously he wasn't going to chicken out. We had to find five penalty takers. He put himself forward and even asked to take the first one.' In his dark blue shirt, Paul Pogba faced up to the Uruguayan keeper to set an example for his teammates and show them the way forward. He tried to expel the pressure by looking up high into the Turkish sky. This allowed him to forget the whistles that surrounded him as he placed the ball on the spot. He started slowly before sprinting up. A diagonal shot that grazed the post. Goal! Now it was up to his teammates to play, the French goalkeeper in particular. Alphonse Areola was inspired. He blocked two of the first three Uruguayan attempts, and the French team won 4–1, taking the crown from the Brazilian team, who had won the title two years earlier.

It was Paul who lifted the precious trophy. He also had his own personal award: Pogba had been voted the player of the tournament: 'I'm happy and proud,' he explained after the match, holding his trophies. 'It's something exceptional. A dream come true. We've made our mark on history. Future generations will talk about us.' Paul left his captain's armband in the dressing room before boarding the bus back to the team hotel. He had become one of the lads again, a moodmaker and joker par excellence. He went from seat to seat in fits of laughter, stirring up the crowd: 'So, guys. Are we world champions or not? Who did you say were the world champions?' The players started chanting again: 'France!'

After his sending off against Spain in March, Paul was not about to miss out on his third chance with the France team. This came with another qualifying match for the Brazil World Cup, played on 10 September 2013 at the Gomel Central Stadium in Belarus. Against a solid team led by Alexander Hleb, Deschamps' players were behind against all expectations, but fortunately, the French broke down Belarus in the second half and imposed themselves 4–2 with a final goal scored by Pogba. Although not everything had been perfect, far from it, Paul had scored points. 'It's clear that he has an impressively strong character for his age,' noted Dimitri Payet after the win. The following matches confirmed this trend. Alongside PSG's Blaise Matuidi, Paul became Deschamps' first choice in midfield.

On 13 May 2014, Didier Deschamps delivered a list of 30 names for the 2014 World Cup on the TF1 stage live on the eight o'clock news: seven reserves and 23 other squad members heading to the home of football. These lucky ones included Paul Pogba… and Antoine Griezmann!

Antoine's first selection had been formalised by Didier Deschamps on 27 February. He was one of seven strikers selected for the friendly game at the Stade de France in Saint-Denis against the Netherlands. On 5 March 2014, Antoine was in the starting eleven. His entire family were in the stands at the Stade de France to savour this magical moment. It was the start of a great love story with Les Bleus. 'The manager had always told me to play freely. But when you hear your first 'Marseillaise' it's not that easy to control your emotions. I almost cried during the anthem,' the new international would recognise some time later. 'I saw my parents opposite me and I had to look up to the sky to make sure the tears didn't come. I was in the starting eleven so I had to deal with it.' He was obviously weighed down against the Dutch. He struggled to free himself and to channel his desire to play, his willingness to show what he was capable of. Antoine played 68 minutes before being replaced by Loic Rémy. It was not enough to score but enough to show some promise on the left wing and a natural understanding with Benzema.

On 27 May at the Stade de France, he started for a second time against Norway, a 4–0 win, failed to score and came off after an hour but was named the best French player of the first half. Five days later, in Nice, he replaced Rémy half an hour from the end of the game against Paraguay. The score was still 0–0. After several fumbled balls, he did not miss his first real chance in the 81st minute and scored his first goal for the senior team. Griezmann was ready for his first World Cup. Brazil here we come!

The start of their first World Cup was encouraging nonetheless. On 15 June 2014, at the Beira-Rio stadium in Porto Alegre, La Pioche celebrated his first appearance in the competition against Honduras by winning a penalty in the 45th minute that led to Karim Benzema opening the scoring just before the break. Antoine Griezmann played the whole match (3–0) and enjoyed his first appearance in the greatest of competitions. He also narrowly missed scoring but his performance on the left wing and widely praised understanding with Benzema and Valbuena had led to the biggest French absentee from the competition, Franck Ribéry, being forgotten.

For the game already being heralded as the group's decider, five days later in Salvador de Bahia against Switzerland, Deschamps had also decided to give Olivier Giroud a start and moved Benzema to the left at Griezmann's expense. The Arsenal striker did not let his first opportunity pass him by: in the seventeenth minute, his diagonal header was accurate and ended up in the top corner. One–nil. Paul was a substitute, but this did not prevent him from making his mark with an assist to Sissoko, shortly after coming on for Karim Benzema in the 67th minute. It was 5–0 to France in the 73rd minute. What a demonstration! Just as Antoine was coming on for Valbuena, the Swiss scored through Dzemali. Xhaka would eventually pull the score back to 5–2.

Despite this, his record was tarnished by his third Group E match against Ecuador. On 25 June at the Maracanã in Rio de Janeiro, Les Bleus disappointed with a lacklustre 0–0 draw against the South American team. Paul was not saved this time by Deschamps, who left him on the pitch until the very end. The comments were unforgiving: adjectives such as 'irritating' and 'self-satisfied' came thick and fast to those charged with writing detailed accounts of the match. Griezmann earned his second start in the World Cup, still on the left wing, and was the most dangerous French striker on the second half. Replaced in the 79th minute, the Sociedad stalwart was one of the few French players not to have disappointed. France qualified all the same and topped Group E ahead of Switzerland.

Over the *RMC* airwaves, Jean-Michel Larqué, a former French international, not only called into question Pogba's performance against Ecuador but also his behaviour in general: 'Even if I'm not with the France team day in day out, I feel that Paul Pogba's attitude means "I'm just as good as the more experienced players." … Paul Pogba's concern at the moment should be keeping his place. He does not behave like a player of his age towards his elders.'

But Paul was on the front line before the decisive last sixteen game that saw France take on Nigeria, runners-up in Group F behind Argentina, on 30 June at the Estádio Nacional (Brasilia). This time he was up to the task. And in style! While France were struggling in the first half, he held firm in the midfield, sweeping up balls and hardly letting anything go. But the first hour of play was dire. Nigeria posed Les Bleus a huge number of problems and the French came close to disaster on two occasions.

Deschamps had to react quickly. In the 62nd minute, he made his first change, replacing Olivier Giroud with Antoine Griezmann. The repositioning of Benzema as a number 9 and his clear understanding with Griezmann allowed the French to be more dangerous. Benzema took advantage of a one-two with Antoine to do what he needed with the ball, sliding it under Enyeama before it was cleared off the line by Victor Moses.

In the second half, in the height of battle, Pogba took on the guise of national hero by breaking the deadlock in the 79th minute: he took advantage of a corner from Mathieu Valbuena that had been badly cleared by Enyeama to head the ball victoriously into the open goal. One–nil. While you might imagine an exuberant celebration, this time he kept his joy inside. He allowed himself to be surrounded by his teammates but showed no reaction. It was as if he did not want to show his anger after the wave of criticism that had broken over him. Les Bleus finished strongly, and, after injury time, Valbuena put in a low cross from a corner played back to Benzema. Griezmann was lying in wait in front of Enyeama but was beaten to it by Yobo, who scored an own goal.

Fourth of July 2014, Maracanã Stadium (Rio de Janeiro). The team that had shone against Switzerland was back. Only Giroud was out of the starting eleven in favour of Griezmann. Deschamps was hoping this would be the team to get the better of Joachim Löw's Germany. Like Les Bleus, Die Mannschaft had been blowing hot and cold since the start of the competition, and eventually made it through by the back door in the last sixteen against Algeria, winning 2–1 after extra time.

In the thirteenth minute, Toni Kroos measured a free kick perfectly for Mats Hummels. At 6ft 3in, the Borussia Dortmund defender got the better of Varane to fire a powerful header under the bar. Goal! Germany 1, France 0. France already had their backs against the wall. They had to react. Antoine was struggling up front, running all over the place and calling for the ball. Paul went down fighting at the Maracanã. The best French player in the first half, he was one of the few to compete with the world champions in waiting and fought throughout the 90 minutes. Only the final whistle could quash his hopes of a World Cup-winners medal. He could console himself with the title of the tournament's best young player, ahead of his friend Raphaël Varane.

Antoine's face finished buried in his blue shirt. He was crying. Varane, Sissoko, Mavuba, Rémy and even the captain, Hugo Lloris took turns in comforting him, but he was inconsolable. 'We could have eaten them for breakfast,' said Antoine a little later, once he had dried his tears. 'A World Cup in Brazil only happens once in your lifetime but it was a great honour to have been with Les Bleus and an important learning experience for the future.'

With Euro 2016 in mind, Paul Pogba and Antoine Griezmann were thought to embody the future as well as the present for Deschamps', which had lost several of its senior players along the way: Karim Benzema and Mathieu Valbuena were taken out of the running by the sex tape affair in October 2015, while Raphaël Varane and Lassana Diarra were both injured at the last minute. 'We won't be able to say whether these Euros belonged to the Pogba–Griezmann generation until they're over,' tempered the Juventus player while speaking to a journalist from *Le Monde* two days before the start of the competition.

Didier Deschamps unsurprisingly picked Antoine and Paul in his starting eleven for the opening match against Romania at the Stade de France on 10 June. The Atlético striker, unremarkable, was replaced in the 66th minute by Kingsley Coman with the score at 1–1. Paul played 77 minutes and the verdict was harsh: 'Lack of precision,' 'lack of solidity,' 'lack of coherence.' Dimitri Payet at least saved Les Bleus' skin in their first match with an uncompromising strike into the top corner in the 89th minute. France 2 Romania 1.

'Concerned about Griezmann' read the title on the front page of *L'Équipe* on 13 June, two days before the match against Albania. 'The expected leader of Les Bleus attack, the Atlético Madrid striker, seemed wiped out against Romania on Friday. Should we be worried?' continued the newspaper. On 15 June, at the Stade Vélodrome in Marseille, both Pogba and Griezmann were on the bench. After half-time, Paul went on for Martial, who had seemed absent for most of the first half, and Griezmann replaced Coman after an hour of play. In the 89th minute, the score was locked at 0–0. Adil Rami set off down the wing. The defender used his stronger right foot to guide the ball. In the penalty area, Antoine jumped up for the header. His touch was spot on as he met the ball on the diagonal before it bounced just in front of the line and went over. GOAL! Antoine just kept on running before shouting a few words in anger. He was eventually caught by his team-mates, sandwiched between those on the pitch and those on the bench. Dimitri Payet scored again in the dying moments of the game. France 2 Albania 0. Les Bleus had qualified for the last sixteen.

Nineteenth of June. First place in the group was up for grabs at the Stade Pierre Mauroy in Lille against Switzerland. Antoine and Paul Pogba had become inseparable. In the dressing room, still wearing the official France team suit, they tried out a few dance steps for the federation cameraman. It was a way of marking their return to the starting eleven and their understanding was equally perfect on the pitch. In the seventeenth minute, Griezmann combined with the future Manchester United recruit, who hit the cross-bar. In the second half, it was Pogba who cleaned up by shouldering his way past three opponents. He passed to Griezmann, who got support from a teammate before forcing the Swiss keeper to scramble to keep the ball out. Ni–nil and Les Bleus topped Group A; the last sixteen would see them take on the Republic of Ireland, who finished third in Group E behind Italy and Belgium.

On 26 June, after just two minutes of play in the last sixteen at the Parc Olympique Lyonnais in Décines-Charpieu, La Pioche committed a foul on the Republic of Ireland striker, Shane Long, inside the box. The Southampton forward played it well and pushed the

French midfielder too far. Penalty! Robbie Brady did not need to be asked twice to wrong-foot the French goalkeeper, Hugo Lloris, and give his team the lead.

Luckily for the French, Grizi decided to play one of the matches of his life. The darling of Atlético Madrid turned the match around by scoring two goals with an hour played. In the 58th minute, Antoine almost missed a ball that came in from Matuidi on the left. With the very tip of his foot, he just managed to knock it on to Coman, who passed it back to him with a single touch. Antoine then looked for Dimitri Payet, on the diagonal, who switched play to the right following a call from Sagna. The Manchester City defender controlled the ball before sending it into the space between the six-yard-box and the penalty spot. Griezmann surged forward, got in front of his defender and brushed the ball towards the far post with his head for the equaliser. This time, when it came to celebrating his goal, Antoine managed to escape Giroud's embrace and he slid majestically across the turf at the Parc OL. For his return to his home region, Antoine had invited his nearest and dearest, getting them seats in the stands. He finished with the lightning gesture made famous by Usain Bolt and puts his thumb in his mouth to dedicate this goal to his daughter Mia.

But his work was not done yet. Just three minutes later, Laurent Koscielny sent a long ball forward towards Olivier Giroud. As he jumped he saw that Antoine Griezmann was already making a move and understood his intentions. Giroud's headed pass was superb. All Antoine had to do was get ahead of his marker and unleash a diagonal left-footed shot that he tucked inside the near post. Goal! In front of the south stand he began a celebration the French fans had never seen before. With his thumbs and little fingers held up to his face he mimed a telephone as his hands and head moved in a jerky rhythm. He would later explain that the dance had been inspired by the video for 'Hotline Bling' by the American rapper Drake. 'I couldn't do it against Albania because it was too emotional. It was the same for the first goal against Ireland, but after the second, I thought it was time and I went for it.'

It was the third fastest double by a French player in a European championship (behind Michel Platini against Yugoslavia in 1984 and Zinedine Zidane against England in 2004). It was also the fastest double in the Euros since 2008.

The joy of the two men was a pleasure to watch. Since the start of the competition, they had seemed inseparable and made their friendship clear in front of the French Football Federation camera. From keepie uppies in training that verged on circus tricks, to NBA PlayStation games and the odd impromptu rap, the duo seemed guaranteed to provide the atmosphere at Clairefontaine. 'We already knew that Paul was close to Patrice Evra, as they had both been at Manchester United and Juventus, but it was during this competition that we discovered his friendship with Griezmann,' noted Grégoire Margotton, a leading pundit for TF1.'

This friendship between the team's two stars was also clear to see on the pitch, especially during France's next two games. When they made short work of Iceland (5–2) in the quarter-final, Paul was completely transformed. He played with freedom, finally ruling the roost in midfield. His passing was good, his tackling unbeatable, his play simple and he scored for the first time in the competition. In the twentieth minute, the Juventus player jumped up into the Saint-Denis night to catapult a header inside the far post on the end of a corner delivered by none other than Griezmann. It was his first goal for France in more than a year and a half. Just before the break, in the 45th minute, he also found himself on the end of a long ball before starting a move that, after a return pass from Giroud, put Grizou through to score.

The duo were up to their old tricks in the semi-final for the revenge match against the world champions. Right before half time, Bastian Schweinsteiger was judged to have deliberately handled the ball in his own area. Penalty! The Stade Vélodrome exploded. It was perfect timing. Just before the break. Antoine placed the ball on the spot to deliver the punishment.

Looking into the emptiness, Antoine focused and was off without hesitation as soon as the referee blew his whistle. Six paces and a clean strike. Manuel Neuer went to his left and Antoine fired the ball the other way, into the bottom of the net. One–nil. He broke into a repeat performance of the Drake celebration, then turned to the touchline and shouted '*Vamos!*' into the pitch-side camera, pulling on his blue shirt.

France had one foot in the final. And then soon a second. In the 72nd minute, Antoine scored his second double of the competition. It all started with some insistent pressing from Pogba, who picked up the ball on the left. The Juventus player, soon to return to Manchester, saw his strike-cum-cross parried by Manuel Neuer. It landed at Antoine's feet, like a gift. He took advantage of the error and scored his second in the 72nd minute! 'Grieeeeeezmann!' screamed the commentator in ecstasy. He was on top of the world. Les Bleus had just beaten the world champions.

The France team would play a home final, just as their predecessors had done in 1984 and 1998. The final would also be all about Griezmann because France's opponents were Portugal. It was manna from heaven for the media who took the opportunity to delve into the maternal roots of the France number 7. They interviewed the directors of Sporting Club de Mâcon (formerly Portugais de Mâcon), where Antoine's father, grandfather, two uncles and now his younger brother Théo played. They also heard from his great aunt, Isabel Silva, who had stayed in the old country: 'Portugal is our team. But I love Antoine. If it's between him and my country, I choose him. I'll be supporting Les Bleus.'

'From the moment we knew who would be playing in the final the whole community was interested in him,' said his uncle, José Lopes. 'But he's never really been immersed in Portuguese culture. He knows and likes Portuguese food but he only went to Portugal once.'

In the pre-match comparison with Ronaldo, the statistics seemed to favour the young French player: six matches each but six goals for Antoine and only three for CR7. The Portuguese player had provided three assists, compared with two for Antoine. Experience was on Ronaldo's side. He had played in the final stages of every Euro since 2004 and was the only person to have scored at least one goal in each of the last four tournaments. He had even joined the Frenchman Michel Platini, the hero of 1984, at the top of the ranking of goal scorers in the competition.

But after just a quarter of an hour of play, Ronaldo lay down in tears on the Saint-Denis pitch. He had been dragging his left leg since a clash with Payet in the eighth minute. He was replaced by Quaresma in the 25th minute. The Griezmann–Ronaldo duel would end there for the time being. 'Despite Ronaldo's exit, it soon became clear that it was going to be very tough for France,' said the TF1 commentator Grégoire Margotton. 'A Euro is so much tougher than a World Cup, especially when it comes to nerves, because there are no easy matches when you can rotate your team.'

During the second half, Les Bleus tried to force the hand of fate with André-Pierre Gignac's golden opportunity at the end of added time. The striker got past Pepe and wrong-footed Rui Patricio, but the ball hit the post. Antoine also had an opportunity to finish it: in the 66th minute, Coman had just come on for Dimitri Payet. The Bayern Munich winger crossed the ball from the left, this time Antoine got the better of Guerreiro with a header, just six yards out, but it went over the bar. It would have been decisive.

In the 109th minute, Eder scored the winning goal with a low diagonal right-footed shot from 25 yards out. It was a terrible way for it to end. After the game, Antoine was like all the French players: stunned, stupefied and dumbfounded. He searched for some support and comfort from his friends and family in the stands. He understood that once again the trophy had been stolen from under his nose. One month after the Champions League final, he had missed out again. Portugal 1 France 0.

Paul would lie prostrate on the pitch at the Stade de France, his first European trophy having slipped through his fingers. He had not been able to provide the touch of genius Les Bleus so desperately needed. 'There is always a huge amount of expectation around Paul,' commented his former manager, Pierre Mankowski. 'Then, when he's not so good, they're quick to criticise him. Sometimes we forget that he's still a very young player.' In France, where Paul was judged harshly, he was likened to 'an intermittent performer' who had had a nondescript tournament, to a player all too often incapable of putting his talent to the use of the team. The Italian press, despite usually praising him highly for his performances in Serie A, were also extremely tough, and *La Repubblica* rubbed salt into the wounds: 'During the final, Paul Pogba missed every opportunity in a match that could have been his consecration.'

For Kylian Mbappé, the incredible 2015–16 season had also been marked by a misunderstanding with the French Football Federation that had dragged on for almost three years: Kylian had not played any official matches for the France U16 team in 2013, had made only two appearances in an U17 blue shirt in September 2014 and then almost nothing. 'Like others before him, Giuntini – then France manager – was annoyed by Kylian's character,' said an insider.

As a result, Kylian would not be called up for the U17 Euros and would eventually find his international status with players born in 1997, since the France U19 manager, Ludovic Batelli, called him up in March 2016 for the last qualifying round of the European Championships.

Kylian was quickly welcomed and soon became indispensable on the pitch. After a first start against Montenegro on 24 March, he made the difference in the two last qualifying games: he opened the scoring from a corner on 26 March during a big 4–0 win over Denmark; yet again, he scored the only goal three days later against Serbia in the decisive match: 'Even though he was almost two years younger than some of the other players, Kylian showed an incredible maturity,' remembers Batelli. 'He was quickly adopted not as the youngest player coming into the group, but as a great player and a great guy in the dressing room.'

Between 12 and 24 July 2016, Kylian brought happiness to the France team during the Euro U19s played in Germany: 'We saw him try some incredible things, like bringing down an opponent with a simple body dummy or pulling off a rainbow kick after a looping flick. He was fantastic throughout the competition,' recalls the journalist Damien Chedeville. 'He was decisive in the group games, with a stunning goal against Croatia and then two in the vital match against Holland, which we won 5–1.' Kylian was also on form during the semi-final in Mannheim on 21 July, when he took the France team through against Portugal.

In the second half, he secured the win for Les Bleuets thanks to two more goals in the 67th and 75th minutes. 'It was in that game that he again showed those who doubted him that there were no limits to the progress he could make,' says the *Monaco-Matin* journalist Fabien Pigalle. On 24 July, France were crowned U19 champions of Europe, thrashing Italy 4–0. Kylian failed to score but it didn't matter, the 2015–16 season had already been more than generous. Records for his age, a first professional contract, the Coupe Gambardella and European champions, everything he touched had turned to gold! Or almost ... Kylian had to wait until September to pass his STMG baccalauréat, for which he had fallen short by nineteen points. Proof that not even he could get everything right first time!

At 10.17pm on 31 August 2017, Kylian Mbappé came on in place of Olivier Giroud. It was the 75th minute of the game and France were 2–0 up against Holland in Saint-Denis, thanks to goals from Antoine Griezmann and Thomas Lemar. At 10.32pm, in the 91st minute of the game, with the score at 3–0, the boy from Bondy scored his first goal in a blue shirt. His devastating pace down the right wing had baffled the orange defender who had no idea where to look. A one-two with his former teammate Djibril Sidibé and a shot with the side of his right foot saw him thread the ball past poor Jasper Cillessen. It was only his fifth cap and his seventh shot on goal. He was the youngest scorer in a France shirt after George Lech, the RC Lens player, who had scored his first international goal against Switzerland on 11 November 1963, aged eighteen years and five months (Kylian was eighteen years and eight months old).

The Pogba–Mbappé–Griezmann era had just started.

Chapter 11

Golden Boys

'Vote Griezmann' said the front page of *L'Équipe* on 20 September 2016. The headline was accompanied by a photo of Antoine wearing the red and white shirt of Atlético Madrid, all smiles, with his hands behind his ears to magnify the sound of the deafening roar of the Vicente Calderón. 'After shining for Atlético Madrid, the French striker has taken on a new dimension this year and set his sights on a place among the top three for the Ballon d'Or.'

'He finished the Euros as top scorer with six goals … he is now France's favourite player by a long way. With thirteen goals in 36 games, he is scoring at a similar rate to Thierry Henry [twelve goals]. He is now hot on the heels of a certain Zinedine Zidane, who was the last French player to win the Ballon d'Or in 1998.'

L'Équipe had thrown themselves into a battle that seemed lost before it had begun. On one side, Cristiano Ronaldo had played in the Champions League and European Championship finals but, unlike Antoine, had won both. On the other, Lionel Messi had won

La Liga and the Copa del Rey with Barcelona. But *L'Équipe* were insistent, buoyed by patriotic sentiment: Griezmann, a French player, could make a nation's dream come true and put an end to years of disappointment by winning a trophy no French player had won since 1998. The daily newspaper also harboured hopes that changes in the method of picking a winner offered Atlético's number 7 a better chance of victory. In 2016, the Ballon d'Or had been handed back to its founder, *France Football,* after the partnership with FIFA had come to an end. It would now be voted for by journalists, as well as national team captains and managers.

The newspaper was not the only one to support the candidacy of the French player. Diego 'El Cholo' Simeone had been doing so for months. Zinedine Zidane failed to play the patriotic card, however, and preferred to vote for Ronaldo, his player at Real Madrid. The result was declared on 12 December. Cristiano Ronaldo won the Ballon d'Or for the fourth time in his career with 745 points. Lionel Messi came second with 316 points and Antoine finished in third place with 198. It was the second time that year that Antoine had come up against Cristiano and lost: the Portuguese player had also beaten him in the race for the title of European player of the year awarded by the continent's sports media.

'I'm finishing behind two "monsters" of the game, two legends,' Griezmann told *France Football* after the ceremony. 'I'm very proud to be in third place.' He had made it to the third step on the podium without winning a single title. It was his goals, quality football and personality that had seduced the jury. In the meantime, he could console himself with an impressive collection of titles won in 2016: top scorer and best player at the Euros, best player in La Liga and the fans' favourite, best French player abroad. Finally, on 20 December, he received the trophy for French footballer of the year awarded by *France Football*.

The awards season was coming to an end. The Best FIFA Football Awards was held in Zurich on 9 January 2017. Erika, elegant in a long dress, accompanied Antoine for the occasion. Wearing a white shirt, black tie and jacket, the French player posed for photographers, bringing out his Drake celebration and telling journalists: 'It's a pleasure to be here. 2016 has been a fantastic year for me. My daughter was born this year. And as for football, I've had some wonderful experiences with the national team and Atlético.' With 7.53 per cent of the votes, Griezmann once again found himself in third place on the podium at the end of the gala.

On 4 December 2013, *Tuttosport* dedicated its front page to Paul, with a huge colour photo, announcing that the young French player had been voted the best young footballer of the year by an international jury of 30 sports journalists. Pogba succeeded Isco, the 2012 winner, on a golden roster packed with illustrious names. He was the first Juventus player to win the junior Ballon d'Or and, like those who had preceded him, he also dreamt of winning the grown-up version.

He talked about it on 4 December at Saint Vincent in the Aosta Valley at a gala event. Looking extremely dashing in a tuxedo, white shirt with a bow tie and gold Mohican, the young French player held up the prize with a smile on his face. 'I'm happy and proud,' he said with confidence. 'When I think back to when I was a child and I wanted to do this job, I wanted to win a prize like this. Now my next objective is to win the other golden ball.'

Who was he dedicating the trophy to? 'To my mother, Yeo Moriba, to my dad, Fassou Antoine, to my big brothers, Florentin and Mathias. And also to my teammates here at Juve, to the club, to my fans and of course to my agent, Mino Raiola … 2013 really has been a golden year for me,' said the twenty year old from Roissy-en-Brie. And it was certainly not going to end there: the 2013–14 season had got off to a great start.

It was 6.50pm on Monday 24 October 2017 when Kylian Mbappé, wearing a black tuxedo, white shirt and bow tie, climbed out of a Mercedes van and went into the Sporting Club in Monte Carlo. He was accompanied by Wilfrid, Fayza and his younger brother, Ethan. The boy from Bondy was back, for one evening, in the city that saw him make his Ligue 1 debut and where he was crowned champion of France.

He was going back to his roots to collect the 2017 Golden Boy award. The PSG rookie had blown away the competition with 291 points, almost double those of the player in second place, Ousmane Dembélé, recently purchased by Barcelona.

He was joining a golden roll of honour that included, among others, the names of Wayne Rooney, Lionel Messi and Paul Pogba. So there he was, smiling, wearing a white Nike t-shirt printed with the number 97005, waiting to receive the entire *Tuttosport* delegation in his Monaco hotel room before the awards ceremony.

Photos, handshakes, autographs and an exclusive interview for the Turin newspaper followed. Le Petit Prince talked about all sorts of things. 'I understand very well that people expect a lot from me in every game, but it's hard for a player to be at their highest level in every match, only the greats manage it. Up to now I've done some great things and if I continue to put in the effort I can do even better. I'm living a dream and I have to take advantage of it and work hard.' He also talked about precocity and his childhood idol: 'Cristiano Ronaldo? Of course, it seems strange that a champion like him never won this prestigious award, but there are some players who mature early on and others who reach their potential later.'

Onto another subject, another example: Thierry Henry. 'I'm honoured by the comparison, but I don't want to be the new Thierry Henry, or the new anyone. I just want to be myself, Kylian Mbappé.' He also talked about his relationship with Neymar. 'It's an honour that Neymar holds me so highly. He knows I admire and love him. And when a player like him takes you under their wing, you have all the credentials you need to progress.'

And so, here was the ambitious eighteen year old in the Salle des Étoiles at Monaco's Sporting club. When his name was called, he left his table and climbed onto the stage to collect the award. Emotional, in front of an audience of 300 invited guests, he received the trophy, a heavy golden ball, from Paolo De Paola, Director of *Tuttosport.*

'I would like to dedicate this to my little brother Ethan,' said Kylian, who could see another gift arriving, a signed Cristiano Ronaldo shirt. Wilfrid, Kylian's father, told the microphones: 'We are very happy. Today is the reward for his talent and all the hard work put in by our family. No, I'm not surprised by Kylian, the only surprise is that it's all happened so quickly. But the things he's doing now he used to do when he was a child, as those who saw him play back then well know.'

France Football unveiled the Ballon d'Or classification on 7 December 2017, with Cristiano Ronaldo, Lionel Messi and Neymar, Paris's new star, in the top three. So far, so predictable; the surprise came with a glance at the top ten. Gianluigi Buffon, Luka Modrić, Sergio Ramos and seventh, with 48 points, Kylian Mbappé! Yet another age record. By just six days, he was ahead of

Michael Owen, the youngest player to be named in the recent history of the award, who came fourth in 1998.

Who would have bet on such a result just a few months earlier? Not even Kylian. 'I really never expected seventh. To finish in the top ten with my first nomination is extraordinary. I'm really starting to enter the big league. I have a lot of respect for all those great players, who I was still watching on TV or playing with on my console not so long ago,' Kylian confessed to *France Football.*

The year 2017 had been his, as even a study carried out by Pressedd showed. Kylian Mbappé was the French sportsperson who had received the most mentions in the media during 2017. His name had come up an astonishing 44,056 times. These statistics were even more astonishing when it became clear that in 2016 the boy from Bondy had been in 219th position.

Chapter 12

Branding superstars

It was clear during the 2015–16 season that Antoine had taken on an extra dimension on the pitch. He had become the new idol of the young who enjoyed imitating his game and his celebrations. He had become the new symbol of a team that had rediscovered its place in the nation's hearts. Every time he appeared on the official website of the France team he created a buzz during the competition, and the video *A Day with Griezmann at Clairefontaine* broke all audience records on the FFF's YouTube channel.

Before Euro 2016, he had been voted to appear alongside Lionel Messi on the French cover of the famous *FIFA 16* videogame. He was also cast in the new marketing campaign for the Beats by Dre headphones brand with Harry Kane, Mario Götze and Cesc Fabregas. But this was nothing compared to the media frenzy that would follow the European Championships. First of all came the magazine front pages. Interest in Antoine now went beyond the sports media: *Paris-Match, Le Parisien Magazine, Sports & Style* and *GQ* took advantage of his new-found popularity to give him pride of place. His exile in Spain had until then kept him at a distance from the wider French public.

Puma, his long-standing sponsor, understood this and played up the personality of its protégé as much as possible. However, in 2014, the sports brand still had him in the background, preferring to use other foot-ballers in its marketing, such as Olivier Giroud. This time, to launch its new deodorant in partnership with L'Oréal, it put the Atlético player on the same foot-ing as its worldwide ambassador, the Jamaican sprinter Usain Bolt. In the advert, the two men run towards each other, face off at a distance and demonstrate the values they share: 'Work, win, celebrate'. The highlight comes at the end: Antoine mimes Bolt's lightning cele-bration after being thrown fully dressed into a swim-ming pool then, the moment of recognition for the Mâconnais player, the fastest man in the world mimics his Drake-inspired moves. It was a *tour de force* by the German sportswear manufacturer, who excelled them-selves with a second version a month later. This time Antoine, all grown up, is on his own. He takes on the guise of cupid for Puma and uses his famous celebra-tion to come to the assistance of budding couples. In a variety of funny situations, he appears as a barman, hairdresser, expert knitter and fighter pilot. During shooting it only took him a few takes to get it right. With his nearest and dearest looking on, he shows the same ease and naturalness on camera as he displays on the pitch. This new version of the advert was launched in November, and, despite coming out so late in the year, became the most viewed of 2016.

After this he was voted 'Man of the Year' by the trendy magazine *GQ.* In the months that followed, he became an ambassador for the Head & Shoulders shampoo brand and Gillette, as his idol David Beckham had once been. He took advantage of this to (finally) shave off his famous moustache: 'I saw the adverts on TV I wanted to be a part of it,' he said when his partnership with the brand was made official. 'My look was never all that important to me. My sister would tell me to pay attention to what I was wearing. You have to be presentable. Take care of your skin, etc.' His look and physical appearance were now key components of the player's marketing.

His social media accounts, gaining hundreds of new fans by the day, revealed his tattoos. A Virgin Mary, a Christ and the initials of his parents on his right arm. The words 'Fame' and 'Hope' as a tribute to his favourite rapper, Chris Brown. He also revealed snapshots of life in his Madrid home: on the sofa watching an NBA game, at a barbecue with friends, or in his car with his girlfriend and dog, Hookie, a cute French bulldog. Antoine was playing in the big leagues.

Sometimes he would lend his face to good causes, such as a campaign to end violence against women. He also lent his voice to Superman in the *Lego Batman* cartoon. The ultimate recognition in France: he almost became one of the performers at the annual Restaurants du Coeur charity concert but had to miss it in the end due to a prior commitment.

The France striker still found some free time to realise a childhood dream. He went back to New York, a city he loves, with the intention of meeting his idol, the American basketball player Derrick Rose. The American playmaker seemed not to know who he was: 'Where are you from?' he asked. 'From France, I've come especially to meet you,' replied Antoine, with no sign of any awkwardness. That's Antoine, modest and always enthusiastic. He brought some gifts for the NBA player, an Atlético Madrid shirt printed with Derrick Rose's number 25. In turn, Antoine did not leave empty-handed, thanks to a shirt signed by his idol and an ovation from Madison Square Garden.

Sixteenth of March 2016, 8.45pm. Juventus were preparing to play a key match in the knockout stages of the Champions League against Bayern. For the first time, Paul Pogba was sporting black and gold boots made by Adidas. Running down each heel of these high-backed boots, christened the 'Ace 16+ Purecontrol', were the words 'POGBOOM' and 'POGBANCE' in large letters. The insole read 'I Am Here to Create.'

Adidas had picked their moment well, taking advantage of this clash between two heavyweights of European football to announce the new partnership through a well-crafted marketing campaign: 'This is the first sponsorship contract I have signed and it was a very important decision for me. I chose Adidas because we are united by our passions and values. Adidas share my dream for a new creative and modern football. I hope to be able to leave my mark and bring something stimulating and new to this iconic brand. The best is yet to come. This is Pogboom! I love music, dance and fashion but my greatest passion is football. I need a brand that gives me the space I need to express myself and explore new frontiers,' La Pioche explained in the press release. According to the Italian media, notably *La Gazzetta dello Sport*, the partnership was said to rest on a €4 million annual deal for a period of ten years.

Adidas were, of course, delighted: 'This is a big coup for us because he plays for a superclub. Euro 2016 is also on the horizon and Paul is expected to be one of the key players in the France team,' said a delighted Benoît Menard, Adidas' director in Paris, in the documentary '*La folie Pogba*'. In the same programme broadcast on *L'Équipe 21* in May 2016, there were those, such as Nouredine El Haoussine (Sports Universal Music and Brands), who were already comparing the Juventus player to a 'rock star like Neymar, more edgy than Eden Hazard and with more star quality than Messi,' and others such as Sébastien Bellencontre (4success), who thought it was a sensational move: 'Given that the player has a showman side and comes across in a relaxed and playful way.' However, this opinion was not shared by Gilles Dumas, a communications expert with Sportlab:

'We all agree that Pogba has value. But this sum just seems amazing to me today. Adidas are taking a gamble. Basically, they're looking for a replacement for Ronaldo and Messi, and Adidas think it might be Pogba.'

The cleverly orchestrated marketing coup became a stroke of genius in the sixth minute of the game against Bayern Munich. Put through by Khedira, the Swiss right-back, Stephan Lichtsteiner stumbled in the German box. The ball fell at the feet of Paul Pogba, who struck a right-footed shot between the legs of the defender Joshua Kimmich and into the bottom of the net deserted by Manuel Neuer. His first Champions League goal of the season.

To secure his golden contract with Adidas, he had had to spend the last few months embroiled in a tough behind-the-scenes battle with his former adviser, Oualid Tanazefti: 'Since November 2014, the player was no longer the owner of his image as he had entrusted the entire 'Paul Pogba' brand to Tanazefti and his associate Ylli Kullashi,' explained an insider. The secrets of the contract ceding image rights were revealed by Mediapart in December 2016, based on documents produced by Football Leaks: for a sum of between €1.8 million and €5 million, Paul Pogba is said to have allowed the Luxembourg company 'Koyot Group', owned by Tanazefti and Kullashi, to recover 30 per cent of the profits on the signing of a new contract, while the two men were already receiving a salary for their work. Paul Pogba would keep 70 per cent of the profits but could not touch the money until 31 October 2029. He would only receive an annual fee of €33,000. Conversely, his representatives would have their hands free for fifteen years to invest the player's fees wherever they wished without justification and recovering half of the profits. Still according to Mediapart, Paul would have to pay back the sum invested at the beginning (between €1.8 million and €5 million) in 2029, while Tanazefti and Kullashi would retain the right to re-sell this image contract without his agreement.

A French insider continues: 'When Tanazefti fell out with the Pogba family and found himself isolated, the image rights contract was all he had left. It was a shame for the kid, who ended up stuck. It was also a way for Tanazefti to have a return on his investment, given that he had been with Paul Pogba since almost the very beginning.' It was only a month later, in December 2014, when Mino Raiola learned of the affair. 'He asked his lawyers to do everything within their power to break the contract and even appealed to the legal departments of some major brands,' continues the insider, who specialises in talented young players. 'He asked Paul to try to negotiate directly with his former mentor to attempt to find an amicable way to recover his image rights. Tanazefti, who did not want to do Raiola any favours, had begun offering the contract to Chinese investors and the Doyen Sports company, and even to Jorge Mendes.'

After the Pogba camp threatened to bring the matter before the courts, negotiations eventually resumed between the two parties. An agreement was finally reached in early 2016: for a fee of €10 million (€6 million for Tanazefti and €4 million for Kullashi, according to Mediapart), Raiola bought back the image rights of his player. According to the Football Leaks documents, the Dutch–Italian agent is believed to have founded a company in Jersey to manage the 'Paul Pogba' brand and it is understood that it was the directors of this company who signed the contract with Adidas. 'This affair has become a case study in football,' says a French sports adviser. 'It shows young people the dangers of this type of contract. A person's rights over their image is a fundamental notion in French law and the athlete must not under any circumstances transfer these rights to a third party.'

While Griezmann went with Puma and Paul chose Adidas, Kylian opted for the other giant: Nike, who have been sponsoring the young centre forward since he was thirteen years old.

Their greatest *coup de théâtre* together came on 14 July, Bastille Day, right when rumours of the possible transfer of Mbappé from Monaco to a bigger club (Real Madrid or PSG) had reached fever pitch. In his room at the Hôtel des Bains de Saillon, Kylian recorded a video message that he posted on Twitter at 9.46pm, captioned 'Grande annonce' (Big announcement). With a serious face and a solemn tone worthy of an important occasion, Mbappé says: 'Hello everyone, it's me. As you know, my name has recently been linked to lots of different things. There have been lots of rumours. I think it's important for me to update you and give you this information. I've thought about it a lot with my family. We've weighed up the pros and cons. We've reached a decision, which is that … this year … from now on … I'm going to play …' Kylian stops to catch his breath. He reaches down and comes back up to the camera holding a pair of football boots. And laughing like crazy, he exclaims: 'In Mercurial Vapors!' It was a publicity stunt for the American company, with whom Mbappé had just renewed his contract, adding a few zeros.

When Kylian finally confirmed his signature for the Nike-sponsored Paris Saint-Germain, the brand also put its hand into its pockets to build a community sports facility: it was opened on 6 September 2017, in the Jardin Pasteur in Bondy, where Kylian scored his first goals. In addition, a huge panel with the effigy of the PSG number 29 also appeared on the side of the eight-storey Résidence des Potagers, also paid for by Nike. This mega fresco looks down from on high over a motorway that spews cars and traffic jams, accompanying the kids that cross the street to go into the Lycée Madeleine-Vionnet and groups of teenagers approaching the Collège Jean-Renoir. In the middle, looking serious and giving a 'shaka' sign, stands Kylian Mbappé, wearing a Paris Saint-Germain shirt. The slogan at the top 'Bondy: the town where anything is possible' pays tribute to the town where Kylian was born.

Chapter 13

Terror

Paris, Friday 13 November 2015

The quarter-final defeat in the 2014 World Cup had stuck in Antoine's throat for a long time, so this friendly match against Germany was timely. It was a chance for revenge, a life-size test for Les Bleus six months ahead of Euro 2016. Unsurprisingly, he was in the starting eleven that Friday night, winning his 23rd cap for the senior team. Strike partners Griezmann and Giroud were joined by the rookie, Anthony Martial, recruited during the summer by Manchester United from Monaco.

The match against Germany took a dramatic turn after the first fifteen minutes of play. The initial explosions near the Stade de France came in the seventeenth and twentieth minutes of the game. Two dull noises could be heard while the play was taking place on the left, the other side of the pitch. Antoine cast an anxious look towards the bench but as play continued he did nothing else.

At almost 11pm, as they walked down the tunnel towards the dressing room at the Stade de France,

Antoine and Les Bleus found out about the night of terror unfolding in Paris: suicide bombers around the stadium, deadly attacks on several café and restaurant terraces in the centre of Paris and the hostage-taking at the Bataclan, where three heavily armed men burst in during a performance by the American group Eagles of Death Metal. Antoine Griezmann immediately thought of his sister. He remembered she was planning to attend a concert in the capital that night. Les Bleus' number 7 quickly got in touch with his mother. She did not know anything. Antoine was increasingly anxious and worried for his sister. As far as Antoine was concerned, there was no doubt, Maud was at the Bataclan. The hours that followed were endless. For security reasons, the two teams had been ordered to remain in the dressing rooms at the Stade de France. Despite the isolation, Antoine continued to gather as much information as possible, calling his parents and brother Théo. His teammates and staff did everything they could to reassure him, but, of course, it was not enough.

At 12.10am, the security forces stormed the Bataclan. At 12.43am, Antoine posted a message on his Twitter account to share his concern: 'Thoughts with the victims of the attacks. God take care of my sister and of the French people. #vive la France'. At 2.55am, Les Bleus were given permission to leave the Stade de France.

At 3.30am, Antoine posted a second message on Twitter, this time to announce his relief: 'Thank God, my sister got out of the Bataclan. All my thoughts are with the victims and their families. #vive la France'. His sister Maud had managed to escape the carnage alive shortly after 1am. When the terrorists first came in she was pushed into a corner of the room and found herself face down on the ground, closing her eyes from time to time to avoid having to see the unbearable. She tried to move as little as possible, to 'play dead' and to stay within reach of her boyfriend, hiding just a few metres away.

When the building was stormed by the security forces, they took off their shoes and ran as quickly as possible, without looking back, to the emergency exit. They spent fifteen minutes running and walking barefoot before they found a taxi.

That night of terror brought the Griezmann clan even closer. A few days after the events, the family took refuge in Antoine's house in Madrid: 'I felt safe at his house, away from the media hype. We're a close-knit family. My mother attaches a huge amount of importance to the love we have for each other. Our closeness has lasted,' Maud Griezmann told *The New York Times*. A few months after this episode, Maud took advantage of her public relations background to become her brother's press officer at the age of 29. Théo, a former video games geek motivated by Antoine, launched a clothing brand, The GZ Brand, a tribute to his brother, at the age of nineteen: 'We work hard together,' continued Maud. 'We never miss an opportunity to get together at our parents' house in Mâcon. Even Antoine.'

The attacks of 13 November 2015 left 130 dead and 413 injured. They changed the lives of thousands of people and made Antoine keener than ever to spend time with his family.

Manchester, Monday 22 May – Stockholm, Wednesday 24 May 2017

At the Manchester Arena, the curtain had just come down on a concert given by Ariana Grande, an all-American pop star beloved by teenagers. Fans, boys, girls and thousands of parent chaperones were streaming out when an explosive device went off in the foyer. The crowd poured out into the street and the neighbouring station. A long night of blood, terror and waiting began in Manchester. There was the desperate ambulance race, the cordon set up by the police, the peoples' solidarity, the search for the missing. Then came confirmation from the police: it was an act of terrorism. The first reports of the attack spoke of nineteen victims and 50 injured. In the end the death toll would rise to 22, with 59 injured; a massacre claimed by so called Islamic State, the worst in the United Kingdom since the 2005 London bombings.

The next day, Manchester was a city in mourning and under siege. In Albert Square flowers, candles and thousands of people amassed for a vigil. Paul Pogba posted 'Peace', followed by these words: 'My condolences to all families of the victims in Manchester and to all families who are losing loved ones in so many countries due to acts of violence.' Messages of solidarity also flooded in from former players such as Éric Cantona, David Beckham and Cristiano Ronaldo. UEFA agreed to the request to cancel United's pre Europa League final press conference, and Mourinho's words of condolence came through the club website: 'We're all very sad about the tragic events. We can't take out of our minds and hearts the victims and their families. I know, even during my short time here, that the people of Manchester will pull together as one. We have a job to do and will fly to Sweden to do that job. It's a pity we cannot fly with the happiness we always have before a big game.'

The following night, the match in the Stockholm Friends arena began with what was supposed to be a minute's silence in honour of the victims of the Manchester attack. Players wearing both red and white and red and blue shirts with black armbands lined up facing one another in the centre circle as the stands fell silent. But the silence quickly became applause, a cry of pride, of defiance: 'Manchester! Manchester!' 'Come on United, do it for Manchester,' read a card held up by a spectator; 'United against terrorism' read a banner behind Sergio Romero's goal.

In front of the defence, alongside Marouane Fellaini, Paul dominated every part of the pitch. He swept up dangerous balls in the midfield, won the duel with Davy Klassen, the Ajax captain, and sent Marcus Rashford into orbit. For once, it was a dream night for the new midfielder, the box-to-box man. He showed this in the eighteenth minute when he gave his team the advantage. Mata supplied Fellaini, who picked out Pogba on the edge of the Dutch area. The Frenchman rediscovered Pogboom and unleashed a bullet with his left foot. The shot took a deflection off the leg of Davinson Sánchez, the twenty-year-old Colombian centre-back. The ball reared up, flew off in an unpredictable direction and there was nothing poor Onana could do. It was certainly a lucky goal but well-deserved given how Pogba had played and would continue to play over 94 minutes.

It was an extremely important goal as far as Mourinho's plans were concerned. The Portuguese manager had set up a trap in the midfield to stop the young Dutch players, giving Paul the opportunity to play in the way that suited him best. Ajax's young players had talent and plenty of good intentions; their passing was attractive and they played well, but there was no bite to their game. Onana had to pick the ball out of the back of his net for a second time in the 47th minute, after a header by Smalling. The game was over.

'We know things like this [the terror attack at Manchester Arena] are very sad, all over the world not only in Manchester, in London, in Paris,' said a barechested Paul Pogba, 'We won for Manchester, we won for the people who died.'

Dortmund, Tuesday 11 April, Wednesday 12 April 2017
Against the Borussia Dortmund of his friend Ousmane
Dembélé, Kylian Mbappé gave a consummate performance on 12 April 2017 in the first leg played at the
Signal Iduna Park. Against the 'yellow wall', as the
imposing Borussia kop is known, he scored in both
halves to help Monaco to a 3–2 win.

Unfortunately, Kylian's first European 'double'
would go unnoticed due to a tragic event: the day
before, as it was leaving the hotel for the stadium, the
Borussia team bus had fallen victim to a bomb attack
resulting in two minor injuries, including one to the
Spanish player, Marc Bartra, whose wrist was wounded.
A club supporter, a German–Russian in his late twenties, detonated three explosive devices as the bus went
past: 'We came close to disaster that night,' remembers
the *Kicker* journalist, Matthias Dersch. 'The match was
postponed until the following day, but the minds of the
players, fans and journalists were all still elsewhere.'

Kylian would pay tribute to his opponents after the
game: 'Of course, we were delighted to have landed
an important blow, but mostly we were really affected
by what had happened. After the explosion, I immediately called Ousmane Dembélé and told him we were
all with him and all the Dortmund players.' These comments were particularly appreciated by the Borussia
fans and would do much to increase his popularity. 'At
the time, we weren't necessarily paying attention, but
watching the game back later we realised the measure

of his performance,' said Matthias Dersch. 'He'd done everything in that first match: won a penalty [missed by Fabinho], tried his luck a number of times and found his way through twice.'

Chapter 14

Numbers

Antoine was seven years old when he discovered the happiness that watching matches on TV, sprawled with his family on the sofa, could bring. Wearing his white shorts and blue shirt that was too big for him, printed with Zidane's number 10, he had his first experience of success as a fan. 'He adored Zidane too but it was David Beckham who was really his idol. He loved his touch with a football, but especially his elegance both on and off the pitch. He had his Manchester United shirt. That's why he now plays in long sleeves and likes to wear the number 7,' confirms Serge Rivera.

Inspired by Beckham, Griezmann has kept a '7' with him throughout his career, even when he debuted with Real Sociedad with the number 27 on his back. The exception: the number 11 that made him European U19 champion in 2010 and that he wore again at the Brazil World Cup in 2014.

Paul Pogba made his debut with Manchester United wearing the famous red shirt, black shorts and the number 42, but for his first two seasons in Turin he had taken the number 6 – the number he usually wore for France – which is sacred to Juventus fans. It was worn by Gaetano Scirea, an out-and-out sweeper who racked up 552 appearances for the team. He was a gentleman foot-baller who had won everything there was to win with Juve and the Italian national team but was tragically killed at the age of 36 in a road accident in Poland on his way home from a scouting mission to one of Juve's UEFA Cup opponents.

During the summer of 2015, and after two seasons in black and white, 50 goals, two league titles, one Coppa Italia and one Super Cup, Carlos Tevez 'The Apache' said a fond farewell to Juve. It was Pogba's turn to take the number 10, previously worn by Platini, Luis del Sol and Alessandro del Piero. Massimiliano Allegri claimed that 'Paul asked for the number 10; he will have more responsibility because it isn't easy to wear that num-ber.' This seemed unlikely in terms of how tough Paul would find wearing it and given that he appeared to prefer the number 6 he wore with France. Paul the Octopus was an unusual number 10: he was not the clas-sic entertainer, captain or team motivator. But he was very popular among the younger generation. He had the most long-term marketing potential, could sell the most shirts and could replace Alex 'Pinturicchio' del Piero in the collective imagination of the Bianconeri.

'Did he feel like a number 10?' Emanuele Gamba asked him in an interview with *La Repubblica.* 'I'm not a number 10 in terms of my position on the pitch. I feel like a midfielder and it's an honour to wear the number of those who've won the Ballon d'Or. It's an important shirt in the history of Juventus and I want to do it proud.'

But it seemed the number 10 really did not work for him. So much so that on 25 October 2005, during a bad streak, Paul turned up on the pitch for a league game against Atalanta with a '+5' written on his back in felt tip pen. It was something Alberto Ferrarini, a motivator from the province of Treviso, had come up with. Let's take a closer look: '1+0+5' makes '6', the number with which the French player had won three league titles and the U20 World Cup. There was more: '1' and '5' together are '15', the French player's birthday.

Whatever the explanation, the boy got over the block caused by the number 10, or the €100 price tag that had been put on him, and went back to playing as he knew best. Back in Manchester, he reclaimed his number 6 and has kept it ever since.

Kylian Mbappé debuted with the number 33 on his back when he stepped out onto the pitch of the Louis II at barely sixteen years of age, and had the number 20 on his back when he first scored for France on 31 August 2017. But his preferred numbers have always been 10 and 29.

The pearl of Bondy chose the number 29 for his first full seasons at ASM and PSG, in honour of the birthday of his little brother Ethan (29 December 2006). With France and during his second season with Monaco, he kept the number 10. Most recently, he surprised everyone when he swapped to the number 7 and started a hashtag, #K7LIAN, which is likely to be his personal brand from now on.

'For a long time, I said that numbers were unimportant and that it was something that only matters on the pitch,' Mbappé told the PSG website in late 2018. 'However, it is an indication of your ambitions – the player you want to become. I keep trying to progress on the pitch and I think that, for me, it was the right time to change number.'

Chapter 15

The star

The star. At last. The one they had been longing for for twenty years. The gold star that sweeps away disappointments, criticism and memories of finals lost. The star that makes you cry so hard you have to bury your face in your blue shirt. They were world champions, just like Zidane and Co. in 1998. They had given France its second star.

But the team had not started well; they almost got the World Cup off on the wrong foot against Australia in Kazan on 16 June. Les Bleus eventually beat the Socceroos 2–1 but had VAR technology to thank. Andrés Cunha, the Uruguayan referee, had failed to spot that the sliding Josh Risdon had taken out Griezmann's ankle rather than the ball. It was pointed out to him and, after seeing footage on the pitch-side TV, he blew his whistle for the first VAR penalty in World Cup history. Antoine made no mistake from the spot in the 58th minute, before being replaced by Olivier Giroud in the 64th minute. The team in yellow went on to equalise before luck came to the rescue of the French, with a deflected own goal scored by Aziz Behich from a strike by Pogba in the 80th minute. Mbappé was also in the starting eleven in the heat of the Kazan Stadium, but he had not been sharp enough in attack and his defensive work had once again left much to be desired.

Five days later, Kylian, Antoine and Paul were included in the France team's starting line-up for their second group game against Peru, which was already to be decisive. In the Ekaterinburg Arena, with its huge stand open to the sky, Kylian, the unpredictable player, finally showed up; with countless little touches and dribbles, offering solutions before scoring in the 34th minute. A strike from Giroud was misjudged by the Peruvian goalkeeper as Kylian surged towards the far post and helped the ball into an empty goal. His fifth goal for the national side saw him give France the 1–0 win and, at aged nineteen years and six months, he had become France's youngest ever scorer in the competition.

France qualified for the last sixteen with a game in hand, but it had been far from impressive. 'What's going on with Griezmann?' was the *Sport* headline, tinged with malice. The French press did not hold back and everyone lamented that Grizi was not the leader they had all been dreaming of.

The final Group C game against Denmark in Moscow on 26 June ended with a soporific 0–0 draw. France secured first place in the group, with Denmark second. Griezmann was on the pitch until the 70th minute, when he was substituted by Fekir. What about his performance? Flat, transparent and inconsistent. Mbappé came on with just twelve minutes left and La Pioche spent the game on the bench. 'France did not threaten at all and will have to show more to beat their next opponents in the last sixteen,' said *Le Monde* at the end. Paul defended his teammates, Griezmann in particular: 'Grizou does very well. He's always happy. It's not because he didn't score that's not the same Grizou. Don't touch my Grizou!'

Didier Deschamps admitted Grizi had got off to a difficult start, but was convinced he would be at his top level against Argentina. But on Saturday 30 June, the nineteen-year-old Mbappé stole the show and sent Leo Messi and his dreams of winning a World Cup home. The Petit Prince flew across the pitch of the Kazan Arena, leaving the Gauchos' defenders in his wake. In the thirteenth minute, he picked up the ball about 30 yards from his own goal, set off on an incredible run, passed two players, left Javier Mascherano standing on the edge of the centre circle and went up a gear in the last 35 yards to get the better this time of Marcos Rojo, pushing the Argentine defender to foul him in the penalty area. Griezmann made no mistake in front of Franco Armani: the keeper went left, the ball went right.

The number 7 rediscovered his touch against Messi and Co., calling for ball after ball all across the pitch, and Paul Pogba played the full game as a defensive midfielder alongside N'Golo Kanté. *Le Figaro* was full of praise: 'Perfect in his finding of Griezmann or Mbappé up front, the Man U player shone for 90 minutes, while fulfilling all his defensive responsibilities.'

Kylian let his talent do the talking again in the 64th minute, when he gave France back the advantage at 3–2, placing the ball out of reach of Armani, and again four minutes later, when he sent his team past the Argentines once and for all with an impeccable diagonal shot with the side of his right foot. It ended 4–3 as Messi bowed his head.

Mbappé received admiration from all over the world, as well as flattering comparisons with Pelé and Ronaldo Nazario. Kylian was not only voted man of the match, he also became the revelation of the tournament on planet football. 'Mbappé chose the day that Messi and Cristiano Ronaldo left the World Cup to start his revolution,' wrote Jorge Valdano for the *Guardian*. 'He burst into footballing history, flattening everything before him. From the first minute, he appeared to be made of wind and steel ... Demonstrating a precision at speed that we hadn't seen since Ronaldo, the Brazilian.'

Kylian became only the second teenager ever to score two goals in a World Cup game. Only the king, Pelé, had achieved such a feat in 1958 in the final against Sweden, and the Brazilian legend took it upon himself to praise the child prodigy: 'Congratulations, @KMbappe. 2 goals in a World Cup so young puts you in great company! Good luck for your other games. Except against Brazil!'

The path to the final was blocked by the Uruguay of Óscar Tabárez and Antoine's mentor Diego Godín. 'Diego is a great friend. I'm with him every day, in the dressing room and on the pitch,' said Antoine. Since his boyhood days at Real Sociedad, he had always had a Uruguayan by his side, helping him. He had also learned to appreciate *mate* and to love and respect Charrúa culture, something he demonstrated on 6 July in Novgorod.

In the 61st minute, France were 1–0 up against La Celeste thanks to a header from Raphaël Varane, when Grizi found himself with the ball on the edge of the area. His central shot was fumbled by Muslera but the ball flew up oddly before finishing in the back of the net. It was 2–0 and the goal was the final nail in the coffin for the comeback hopes of a tired Uruguay. The French fans in the stands made merry but Grizi chose not to celebrate the goal out of respect for his Uruguayan friends.

The semi-final would not be an easy prospect. France faced Belgium, who had sent O Rei Neymar's Brazil packing against the odds. Things did indeed seem very tough to begin with: no one could keep Eden Hazard quiet, Mbappé was well shackled, even picking up a yellow card for an unsportsmanlike act against the Belgians, and it was not Griezmann's day. But then, again, a French defender stepped up, and this time it was the turn of Umtiti to solve the equation. A header from a corner that was covered poorly by Marouane

Fellaini and the goal came six minutes into the second half. Then it was everyone back to defend Les Bleus' 1–0 lead tooth and nail.

Two days before the final against Croatia, who had just beaten England (2–1), Antoine Griezmann had said: 'I want the star and if I get it, I don't care how!' He may have won the Golden Boot at Euro 2016, scoring six goals, but he had lost the final. As he explained, with a smile: 'I was top scorer but we still lost. So I said to myself: "I'll score fewer goals to see if we win this time."'

Grizi explained it well in the press conference on the eve of the final: 'In our style of play and with the players we've got, defence is the most important thing. We can make something happen with our strikers, Kylian on the break, Olivier with a cross or me, with a little bit of madness, as happens from time to time.' Was he proud that people were now talking about the Griezmann Generation? 'I'm sure I'll be proud later on, but I always put the group first. You can't do anything without the group.'

During the team talk before the game, it was Paul Pogba's turn. He spoke calmly, looking his teammates in the eye and lifting his right hand to emphasise his point by waving his index finger:

'We all know where we are, we all know what we want. We know how far we've come. We know it in our hearts and our eyes, we're focused. Boys, we mustn't forget, and maybe I'm repeating myself. We're 90 minutes away from making history. Ninety minutes. One match. We've played I don't know how many matches in our lives. But this is one match that's going to change everything ... I want tonight to stay fixed in the memory of all the French people watching us. Their children, their grandchildren, even their great-grandchildren. We've got 90 minutes to go down in the history books ... I'm not going to shout, I want us to go out onto the pitch like leaders, like warriors. And afterwards, I want to see tears, not tears of sadness but tears of joy as we're kissing the pitch.'

And that was exactly what happened on Sunday 15 July at the Luzhniki Stadium in Moscow. Griezmann, like Zidane on 12 July 1998, was the best of Les Bleus. He made the difference when France were put under the cosh by the Croatians, led by Luka Modrić and an Ivan Perišić who was playing like a man possessed. Antoine's left-footed free kick was deflected into the goal by Mandžukić. They had failed until then to create even one scoring opportunity yet, thanks to Grizi, Deschamps' boys found themselves in the lead in the eighteenth minute. He also put them back in front after Perišić had levelled things up. He did not allow himself to be put off from the penalty spot by Subašić's fidgeting in the 38th minute. It was his third penalty and fourth goal of the World Cup.

In the first half, Kylian Mbappé had very few touches as he was closely marked by the Croatian defence. Modrić and Co. had understood that the lanky PSG player was France's number one attacking danger. And they were not wrong, as with the few balls that came to him, Kylian seemed capable of making a difference every time. This did not escape Didier Deschamps. Despite being 2–1 up at the break, the French manager urged his team to rely more on its number 10 and to make better use of his calls into space. The effect was immediate.

In the 59th minute, Kylian picked up a deep ball, made it into the penalty area, wrong-footed Ivan Strinić and succeeded at the end of his run in sliding the ball back to Griezmann, who released Paul Pogba. The Manchester United midfielder scored with his left foot on his second attempt. Three–one. In the 55th minute, Lucas Hernández ran down the wing before crossing to Kylian, who was camped out in the centre of the pitch, about 25 yards from the goal. For once, he had time to control it, to look up and check the position of Danijel Subašić and to tuck a right-footed shot just inside the post. Four–one, the Paris striker had put the final out of reach. Lloris's error that resulted in Mandžukić reducing the deficit would not bring the result into doubt (4–2). Twenty years after Zizou's generation, the French team were crowned World Cup champions again.

Kylian finished the tournament with four goals and the trophy for the best young player. He can take his place alongside King Pelé, the only other teenager to have ever scored in a World Cup final. Antoine was the FIFA Man of the Match in the final and for Paul it was a dream end to what had been an up-and-down season.